of Women and
Advertising

JOHN S. STRAITON

of Women and
Advertising

McClelland and Stewart

Copyright © 1984 by John Straiton

McClelland and Stewart Limited
The Canadian Publishers
25 Hollinger Road
Toronto, Ontario
M4B 3G2

Canadian Cataloguing in Publication Data

Straiton, John, 1922-
  Of women and advertising

Bibliography: p.
ISBN 0-7710-8309-2

1. Advertising. 2. Women consumers. I. Title.

HF5821.S76 1984   659.1   C84-098255-0

Printed and bound in Canada by
T. H. Best Printing Company Limited

TABLE OF CONTENTS

READ THIS INTRODUCTION

I have had the devil of a time thinking of a title for this book. The idea for the book itself came when I was lunching with Colleen Dimson, a publisher, and Ethel Teitelbaum, who worked with me and who insisted that I should write a book about advertising. "People think you're an expert if you write a book."

The question was *what* to write about advertising. David Ogilvy had explained the rules of the game in *Confessions of an Advertising Man* and has struck again with *Ogilvy on Advertising*. Jerry Goodis had caused a mild flurry with his (unanswered) *Have I Ever Lied to You Before?* Rosser Reeves smartened me up about creativity with *Reality In Advertising*. George Lois's wild and woolly illustrated story of his adventures in advertising is stimulating and entertaining. I had no desire to rehash these subjects.

As lunch progressed, these women attacked me about the many sins of advertising - "Why is there so much sex in advertising?" "Why are women portrayed as idiots in TV commercials?" "Why are men announcers used to talk to women?" I gave my answers to a lot of the questions as reasonably as I knew how. At the end of the lunch, Colleen Dimson said, "There's your book."

So, as nearly as I can approach it, I have set out to explain advertising from the consumer's point of view, and, as you will discover, the woman is the chief decision-maker/consumer in our society. I have tried to write a sort of *Fodor's* or *Michelin Green Book* guide to advertising.

Bernard Shaw's title, *The Intelligent Woman's Guide to Socialism and Capitalism*, said fairly accurately what I wanted to say, if one replaced the words "Socialism and Capitalism" with "Advertising." But I felt that in the 1980's it might not be perceived as amusedly as it was in 1928. *Love, Mother, Free and Piles* was a title I toyed with, using four of the most powerful words in advertising. Nick Steed, then editor of *Quest Magazine*, suggested *The Selling of Women.* This seemed the closest to what I intended and had a bit of curiosity value for the bookstore racks. But my publishers and others felt it misleading. Many women friends read the rough manuscript, but none suggested an apt title.

Finally, I was sitting on my dock in Muskoka, trying to finish this book, when a neighbour, Jimmy Antonacci, dropped by in his aluminum boat and asked what I was doing. I explained the purpose of the book and he said, "You mean, *Of Women and Advertising?*" So there you have the title.

Of course, I have other purposes in recording some of my beliefs and accomplishments in advertising. Advertising is an ephemeral business. Today's great newspaper ad is used to wrap tomorrow's fish and chips. I have read of Tibetan lamas who sit by a stream with moulds of the Buddha with which they "imprint" the water thousands of times, each being a prayer to the diety. Considering the evanescence of advertising, I have thought a book on the subject might be titled *Printing on Water*. It gives me some pleasure to feel that by telling you about some of the thoughts and images I have worked on, they will not flow away invisibly into the past.

This is not a textbook on advertising. While there is the occasional nod to the methods and work of competitors, I have tried to illustrate my arguments with examples whose results I know because I worked on them. There are many good textbooks on advertising. You will find some of them listed in the bibliography.

This is a book about the kind of advertising I have found to work and why I believe it is in the best interest of the consumer. I hope my largest audience will be among women generally. They are the target of most advertising but usually do not have clear ideas of the workings of the business. Competitors may have some curiosity about what I say (enough to pay for a few copies, I hope). Few of them will be amused. People who manufacture and sell things could get an idea or two and use them to prod their agencies. Perhaps my ideas will even persuade a few of the people who make advertising - in agencies and in the advertising departments of newspapers, radio and TV stations, magazines, and retail stores - that advertising can be rational, factual, and effective ... and *not* hyperbolic.

Some people may be annoyed by what I say. Oversimplification, for one thing, can be annoying. But advertising aims at *masses* of people, and the research that helps to shape the advertising seeks to discover what those masses want and need. Generalizing, then, is part of the craft of advertising. Similarly, because I am a man talking about women, I expect a certain amount of reaction from that direction. Yet, right or wrong, I believe that I at least have had more experience in selling to women than any other person practising advertising today.

In this treatise you will encounter familiar names for which I have conceived important campaigns: Lipton, Good Luck margarine, Noxzema, Blue Cheer, Birdseye, Neet depilatory, Ban, Minute Rice, Coffee Crisp, Aero, Kit Kat, Smarties, Campbell's soups, 'C' Plus orange drink. If you use any of them now, it is quite possible that at some time in your life you were persuaded that they are good products by my words and pictures.

Of course, there is the fond hope that some company president will read this book and say, "By golly, that chap has his head screwed on the right way. I'm going to hire him to advertise *my* products."

Above all, I hope you will be *amused* by much of what I have to say. If we ever take advertising too seriously, we're in real trouble.

CHAPTER 1

Advertising and Women and Women in Advertising

Advertising is the witchcraft of the twentieth century. It has its incantations, its how-to recipes - "eye of newt, and toe of frog, wool of bat, and tongue of dog" - its priests and priestesses, its temple whores and secret languages. Like aspirin and divining for water with a willow fork, advertising works sometimes, and nobody quite knows why. The practitioners and the laity have built up a body of myth and fact.

It is my intent to lay to rest some of the myth, reveal some of the realities, and, in the course of doing so, improve your understanding of advertising. There is no need for you to be the helpless victim of advertising, like some abject victim of a voodoo curse. There *is* something you can do about advertising. But before you can react intelligently, you have to understand how advertising works. Like many of the mysteries of magic, it is all really rather simple.

Advertising is here to stay. This little handbook is *not* a defence of advertising but an attempt to explain its anatomy so you can react to it intelligently rather than emotionally. If I can reduce, even slightly, the ferocity of the attacks I suffer from women, cynical students, and disdainful professors, I will have performed a service to the nation's blood pressure.

How Women Dominate
the Consumer Economy

Allow me to begin by stating my major thesis about the forces that govern advertising: wittingly or not, consumers, most of them women, dominate the Canadian (and North American) consumer economy. Women buy more than 80 per cent of all consumer goods sold. They spend about 70 per cent of the $80 billion that go for consumer goods. Just about everything I know about advertising I've learned from women, because most of the advertising I have made has been created to change women's minds.

My Sears catalogue has about 1,000 pages: 800 pages sell products that women ultimately decide on - clothes, dishwashers, kids' things, furniture. Men's products - tools, hernia belts, and such - occupy about 200 pages. Of the $80 billion or so in retail sales in Canada about $60 billion are made through stores where women are the primary customers. Among products and services that are advertised, women's decisions are about all that counts. My advertising life has been dedicated to understanding this enormous buying force.

A group of magazines hired interviewers to talk to 2,300 wives and 1,700 husbands to find out which had more purchasing influence. Baby food, detergents, furniture polish, perfume are 90 per cent decided on and bought by women. Tea, coffee, cereals, frozen foods, meats, soups, indeed all foods studied except fast food, were decided and bought by women 70 to 80 per cent of the time. In a study on tomato sauce conducted in 1983, we found that almost all purchases and brand decisions for that product were made by women.

Women decide on and make about half the purchases of photographic film and still cameras. The purchase of clothes, dryers, ranges, blenders, vacuum cleaners, and such is determined, most of the time, by women. (Men gather information. They read all the text in those refrigerator brochures and ads.) In choosing black-and-white TV sets women are allowed half the decisions, but when it comes to colour, men take over - 70 per cent decide on the brand. Broadloom, mattresses, and kitchen vinyl are over 70 per cent women's decisions. With family cars, at least a third of the time the brand decision is dominated by the wife. And increasingly, women are buying their own cars. God help the car-maker who doesn't supply an automatic shift. Women make 42 per cent of gasoline purchases, usually deciding the brand.

Most consumer dollars are spent in retail stores where women make most of the buying decisions. Retail advertising usually picks up where the makers' advertising leaves off.

MAKER: "Fluffy detergent contains fabric softener."
SUPERMARKET: "Fluffy detergent, $4.95."

As you can see, retailers do not need to use as much text as manufacturers. This is one of the major sources of disagreement when advertisers talk to storekeepers, who insist that "All you need to say is what you're selling and the price." Complaints about misleading advertising are stirred up mostly by retail ads, which is not surprising since there are so many retail stores - 42,000 food stores alone, and 15,000 or so furniture stores.

Among the hundred largest advertisers are big chains like Sears, Simpsons-Sears, Dominion Stores, Eaton's, McDonald's, Woolworth. Eaton's has more people in its Toronto advertising department than most advertising agencies have. The chains, while frenetically competing with prices, try to build personalities for themselves. Dominion's "It's mainly because of the meat," a selling line that lasted a generation, was changed recently to say "You'll love us for more than the meat."

Most big chains have made for them such products as canned apple juice and instant coffee, on which they slap their own store name. And then there are the no-name brands, notably Loblaw's. They tell the world they cut costs by not advertising and cheap labelling while spending more on advertising than many famous brands. Some prophets see the day when the big chains will become the main makers of foods and household products with national advertisers atrophying like the appendix. Fortunately, women do not seem to be herded quite so easily. The mass supermarkets are feeling the competition as specialty butcher shops and cheese shops and produce markets enjoy a renaissance. The chains strike back with hived-off specialty shops under their vast roofs - Ziggy's, gourmet shops, and such.

The one form of retail advertising that has dwindled, in choice of companies at least, is catalogue selling. When Eaton's dropped out of this huge market, Sears benefited. When the Hudson's Bay Company amputated its gouty Shop-Rite catalogue division, Consumer's Distributing could only grow healthier.* A growing number of specialized catalogues and individual offers may take a lot of business from retailers. And if they ever get the two-way TV communication right, catalogue selling and other retail businesses may take a dramatic turn. But do not count on it. They have been promising in-home shopping for twenty years and more.

---

* We were the advertising agency for Shop-Rite. Sales were increasing and profits were in sight when The Bay decided to close the chain. We heard the news on the radio.

12

Some retailers in the States predict that electronic buying will account for 20 to 40 per cent of purchases. But I share with other retailers a belief in the need for "hands on" shopping. "People like to touch, see, feel, and try things on," says one. And the consumer is a social animal. It is great fun to get out and rub elbows with other shoppers. "How I hate shopping," says Helen, as she makes her third unnecessary sortie of the week into the battleground of the Dominion and Simpsons. The shopping mall is the village square.

In the supermarkets roughly 40 per cent of the shoppers are men. Most of these are married or living with a woman. When I advertised Arrow shirts women bought 70 per cent of the shirts but the men made the brand decision. I find it unlikely, so far, that many of the married or live-in men would be making the buying decision very often: "Why did you get Fab, you idiot? You know we always buy Tide."

In the supermarket, one in five of the men over twenty will be single, with a small number of these either divorced or widowers (and you know where *they* learned about products). If latest guesstimates are valid, 10 per cent of males are homosexuals and they, too, must wash and eat. These are mere figures, of course. They don't measure the reasons men buy macho cars, Marlboro cigarettes, or St. Laurent ties - all of which may be chosen, in part, to impress women.

Listening to Women Talk about Products

In my quest to understand women, I have, over the past twenty-five years, talked with thousands of them about things I have written advertising for, like Campbell's soups and Mulveney's Mother's Friend. I have watched women, in groups of ten or so, chatting about Jello desserts, pantyhose, chicken noodle soup, and horse racing, a total confessional of 3,000 and more.* I have followed readership studies of *Reader's Digest*, *Time*, women's magazines, and daily newspapers, telling how tens of thousands of women respond to advertising. I have learned the reactions of myriad women to television commercials for products like Ban and Black Magic chocolates, by showing them to one woman at a time, to groups, or by telephoning them the day after the commercial has appeared. And I've listened to Helen, with whom I live and to whom I am married.

I learned to cook so I could invent recipes for Borden's Eagle Brand milk, Lipton's onion soup mix, and KLIM powdered milk. I have washed

* These group interviews are often conducted in interview parlours complete with one-way mirrors where copywriter, account executive, and client can watch and hear your comments. Don't pick your nose. If you primp in the mirror, you may by looking directly into the eyes of your seducer.

towels for New Blue Cheer, bathed in Softique, cooked on a Moffat range, mixed and matched Campbell's soups, stirred soft drinks into Whip 'n' Chill, sautéed with Good Luck margarine, and had a weight-loss race with Helen for Metrecal. I have never tried wearing Casbah pantyhose, but I did direct the advertising that introduced Johnson & Johnson's Carefree tampons in Canada.

The People Who Work in Advertising – How It Happens

I sort of ricocheted into advertising. My first job was the result of a client, who owned the paper mill in Kapuskasing, Ontario, twisting the agency's arm. The agency was Spitzer and Mills. After a token six months they fired me. A few years ago they offered me what must have been, at that time, the highest salary for a creative person in Canada. I was having too much fun at Ogilvy & Mather at the time to take it. I have never worked for money. Working for the fun of it has yielded sufficient income for my needs.

When I started in advertising, getting a job was easy, which is probably why so many incompetents were in it in the fifties and sixties. Today it is easier to pass through the needle's eye than it is to squeeze into the advertising business. Every year I see dozens of hopefuls, curiously enough, mostly women, who want to enter our dubious profession. My first advice to them is to try something more respectable like credit collection or punch-press operating. In a recent study ranking the respectability of professions, advertising was listed second from the bottom, undercut only by politicians.

I have to admit that if some genie gave me another crack at life, I would probably choose an advertising career again. In advertising, you are always face to face with the real public. Every day is different. You work with some of the most intelligent, witty, and inventive people you will find in any profession. Advertising is entirely a business of brains. Fairfax Cone of Foote, Cone & Belding Agency, said, "My inventory goes down on the elevator every night." And advertising *does* pay well. It is certainly a business in which women have been able to hack out a place for themselves. More so than any other I can think of.

How People Get to Work in an Agency

It is tough to advise people how to get into advertising. Some people walk in with no experience, hit the right note, and get hired on the spot. Others pound doors for months, years. Most give up.

I have two methods I suggest to innocents looking for an advertising job. Method #1 is based on the probability that on any one day there will be very few openings. Suppose there are 200 good agencies in Canada and on the average each has one copywriting vacancy in a year. Spread that over the 200 working days in a year and you'll see that on an average day in Canada there might be *one* copywriting job open. To be there, in the agency's awareness on *the* day they need *that* writer, you have to cover over *two hundred* agencies. It is not enough simply to leave a résumé. Call, call, call, and yet again call. Use direct mail. Not just one letter, a series. Attach your picture to every message to aid memory. Ask everyone who interviews you to recommend three other people you might call upon. You can usually use your adviser's name and so get to see a higher level in another agency than you would by going through channels. Make a list of the ten places you like best and concentrate on them. When you get a job, wherever, let the top ten know. You may want to step up some day.

Method #2 is what secret intelligence operations call the "mole" approach - burrow from within. Get a job, any job, in an advertising agency and promote your cause. You can choose whether or not to announce your intentions when you seek a position, or you can slip in, a vixen in ewe's clothing, and let people know where you want to go once you've decided. There are a number of jobs in an agency in which you can apprentice, survey the opportunities, make friends, and learn about the business: filing clerk, media estimator, projectionist. I think the best is secretary* or even typist. Don't groan. You'll be learning the business. If you are good you will work with and learn from the top people. One of my secretaries, Barbara Parker, became a copywriter. After writing powerful advertising for Softique bath oil, Rowntree's Dairy Bar, and Campbell's soups, she ran off to be a homemaker. Another, Joanne Ferriman, turned into a TV producer and later a "brand man" in a drug products company. I have had poor luck at keeping secretaries.

My first secretary at Young & Rubicam was quite remarkable - a letter-perfect typist (essential for typing copy) but also very willing, the type of person who gets coffee for you any hour of the day, works through lunch without a squawk, and runs errands that you don't have time to handle yourself. This gem of efficiency was also quite physically attractive and, not yet married, was actively pursued by others in the office. Finally, ambition got the best of my hard-working helper and the next step was a transfer to the traffic department, followed two years

---

* When I met David Ogilvy's older brother, Francis, who ran Mather and Crowther in London, I commented on the number of attractive women in the office. "Oh, we find that women who care for their appearance are more careful about other things as well," he said. I was impressed with this common-sense view and mentioned it to David Ogilvy. "That's just Francis's excuse for hiring pretty girls."

later by promotion to assistant account executive and then full account executive for our clients, Goodyear and Cluett, Peabody (Arrow shirts). Today my former secretary owns and runs a group insurance consulting firm under the name W. R. Shaw, but his friends call him Bill.

Jill Wade shuffled papers in the traffic department at Ogilvy & Mather until we made her head of television production. A French department secretary, Louise Clinton, became the head of the television production department. She is the best in the business and now runs her own production company. An assistant in TV production when I knew her has created a company called Just Testing to make rough commercials for research needs. Her name is Lorna Lambert. One woman, Mary Lynn Skelton, screened TV commercials for me and then became a copywriter. She has a family today and still freelances. A receptionist, Heather Petri, also became a copywriter. An assistant secretary moved into research in Ogilvy & Mather. Marion Plunkett is today one of the most respected research directors in Canada. She is quoted back to *me* about research. A woman who started as an agency secretary headed Ogilvy & Mather's French department in Montreal and was strong contender to be president there. Today, Jackie Grenier is president of her own Montreal advertising agency.

If you want to work in advertising, prepare for a long siege, pray for luck, and do not discourage patrons. I was helped up some big steps in my early days by a couple of people who made me their protégé. I work out my debt by trying to aid today's crop.

Currently, the advertising industry is imploding. Budgets are not increasing as quickly as salaries. Agencies are squeezing their talented people for more and more productivity and they have little time to train new employees. They want experience, specific experience to do *this* job *now*. Cockfield Brown, one of Canada's largest, most respected agencies, has disappeared in an attempted takeover, leaving hundreds jobless.

The women I have known in the advertising business have usually been more interesting than the men. In the time when I became a creative director, men were universally what I believe are today called "male chauvinists." In the movies in those days, women in business wore hats like Hedda Hopper, especially in advertising. I interviewed a Rosalind Russell-type wearing a particularly intimidating hat. The fertility rate was very high in the fifties, and one ran the risk of devoting a lot of time to training a woman writer only to lose her to domesticity. I asked boldly, "How do I know you're not going to get pregnant?" She said, "There are two reasons why I won't, and my husband has both of them."

I can recall many dull men in advertising but no dull women. One prim person who avoided telling me she was vacationing in the Virgin

Islands, because I might tease her, was having a nice affair with a client. (Not recommended.) Another highly inventive sprite gave no quarter to loud, arrogant men, of whom there are too many in advertising. "When I have to, I fight like a cornered rat," she said.

At a meeting of the Toronto Copy Directors' Club, I met Mary Wells, head of Wells, Rich, Green, while she was still anonymous. I had been hired just two days earlier to work at Ogilvy & Mather by Joel Raphaelson, a devoted disciple of David Ogilvy's. Joel said, "A young friend of ours is going to Canada to talk to your Copy Club." He described her briefly. When I met her I said, "Joel Raphaelson says you are very arrogant." She looked at me a second or so and said, "All you Ogilvy people are alike."

Three women who helped me look good by creating effective advertising are Pat Harvie, Robin Field, and Marjorie Deans. Two who worked with me to create Canada's first energy conservation campaign have gone on to greater things - Nancy Bottomly (Lanyon) is today editor of *Avenue* magazine; Susan Munroe is a public relations expert with Gulf Canada. Almost all of the women I have worked with in advertising have continued to be successful and happy. Some have created families. Others have risen to high levels in creative and executive jobs.

The Consumer Creates the Advertising

I learned the most about the mechanics of advertising at a small agency called Tandy. Its founder was a relative to Jessica Tandy. There I wrote copy for electric cattle fences, a book publisher, a popcorn company, a radio manufacurer, corn salve, an aerosol bug bomb, chiropractors, tape worm remedy, and a diaper rinse. (Daisy Diaper Dip was so astringent it may account for a "tight-assed" generation of Canadians.) I also made many of the drawings, acted as the agency's salesman (called "account executive"), wrote tiny radio shows and supervised their broadcast, and decided on where advertising should appear.

From Tandy I went to Young & Rubicam, even then one of the world's great agencies. There I learned from the work of George Gallup what women read and look at. Gallup had been brought in by Raymond Rubicam, advertising genius, to study consumer behaviour. While I was learning so was a Gallup employee, David Ogilvy. Ogilvy eventually hired me to write copy for the new branch of his advertising agency in Canada. I learned to use the Young & Rubicam research findings to lure more women to look at my ads and to read what I had to say. Two years in a row, I got the highest number of readers per dollar in Canadian magazines by Starch Readership measurements. My ads were always near the top in attracting women readers.

The Bridgeport Brass Aerosol bug bomb was the first of its kind in Canada. Tested in the tropics during World War II, it used DDT. You had to take it back to the store for a refill. My dead-fly border was not pretty, but it told the story. Not well enough, though, for the bug bomb eventually bombed.

At Young & Rubicam I gradually became vice-president, when vice-president meant *number two*. I did not so much depart from Y&R as it departed from me. One writer said, "You were part of the bricks." The discipline that had attracted me, like most disciplines, was rejected by my fellow practitioners.

In 1961 I abandoned the safety of Young & Rubicam and joined the skeleton crew of Ogilvy & Mather, just starting in Canada. I was mighty scared about the whole thing, cutting loose from one of Canada's foremost agencies to join a tiny outfit with a reputation for *small* successes. Ogilvy the man did not help. I had shown him my works, among them some smart-alec ads for a dubious line of Canadian wines. At dinner, Ogilvy made a grand show of ordering a bottle of the wine, *and sending it back*. I was utterly baffled by what, years later, I realized was a kind of Scotchman's joke about the dismal quality of the Canadian wine. At the time it simply worried me.

Our first account was Shell. Riding on Ogilvy's reputation, we soon added Bristol-Myers, Rowntree, Schweppes, Pepperidge Farm, Campbell, Metrecal. Eventually the agency grew under us, until I became president, and later, upon Andrew Kershaw's assumption to head the New York office of Ogilvy & Mather, I became chairman of the board and chief executive officer, a title not nearly as cumbersome as the job.

While I worked at Ogilvy & Mather it clearly dawned on me that most of the advertising we created was designed for women. I came to realize that the true creative directors of the agency were the consumers who bought our products. Our research was conducted mostly with women who, in most cases, were married and had children. Our group interviews, our TV commercial tests, our concept tests were done in supermarket parking lots and in shopping centres where we could easily find women. Gradually I came to realize that, in selling goods to consumers, we were at the mercy of the whims and attitudes of the nation's women. And more, since most raw materials - steel to build office buildings, pipelines, cars; trees to build houses and to make newspapers to carry advertising; oil and gas to heat homes and run cars and transport trucks - eventually end up being affected by consumer buying, too. Thus is my life and my life work dominated by women and their buying decisions.

CHAPTER 2

Are You "Average"?

Advertising is shaped by the way women respond to it - you and a hundred million others. Advertising that works survives. Advertising that does not work dies.

Some advertising campaigns, such as Madge the manicurist soaking her innocent victims' fingers in dishwashing detergent or the Dove vs. soap dryness test, can last a generation. The Hathaway shirt eyepatch is still used after more than twenty-five years. I have used a single commercial for a year or more for Rowntree's Coffee Crisp candy bar, Campbell's chicken noodle soup, and Softique bath oil. Other campaigns die in a few weeks or months. The bulk of this book will explain the effects of natural selection on the specious. What must be agreed upon first is the climate in which this struggle for survival is taking place. Who is this "average" person whose response determines what advertising will prevail?

Who Is the Average Woman?

One thing is certain - hardly any of the women reading this book are "average." Reading any book puts a person, man or woman, in a minority. If you can read at all, you are not among the 20 per cent or so of adults reported to be functionally illiterate. One-third of Canadians have not made it past grade nine. Another third don't get beyond grade eleven. Only one in five finishes high school. Reading books is not a common pastime.

If you are reading this right now, you are very likely well above the "average" with whom much advertising must communicate to work.

You Can't Duck This Question Mother...

Does the daily diaper chore take too much time? Well, try Rock-A-Bye Diaper Wash. All you do is dip, swish and rinse... and they come out sweet clean and white.

Rock-A-Bye Bottle Wash is another time-saver ... bottles sparkle in just a moment. And try Rock-A-Bye Baby Soap, so sweet, so mild, made specially for baby's tender skin.

It's for Baby
Buy Rock-A-Bye

Boy-Did I Stick My Neck Out!

Here I always thought diapers needed soaking to be clean. Then along comes Rock-A-Bye Diaper Wash that washes diapers in a few minutes, leaves them clean and white without the slightest scrubbing. It only takes 4 teaspoons per day.

What's more, I find that Diaper Wash is only one of a long line of Rock-A-Bye Baby Products. Mothers love Rock-A-Bye Baby soap; kind to the softest skin.

Ask for Rock-A-Bye Diaper Wash. It's economical.

If it's for Baby ... Buy Rock-A-Bye.

18-Day Supply 39¢
At all Drug, Dept. and Grocery Stores

Hereby Hangs a Tale...

It's the story of a mother who washed Baby's diapers the hard way ... till she found Rock-A-Bye Diaper Wash. Now she does them in a jiffy ... just swish and rinse in active Diaper Wash solution.

And Diaper Wash is only one of a long line of Rock-A-Bye Baby products. Another timesaver is Rock-A-Bye Bottle Wash ... whisks out milky film without scrubbing or boiling, leaves bottles sparkling bright. And don't forget Rock-A-Bye Baby Soap for tender baby skin.

It's for Baby
Buy Rock-A-Bye

At all Drug, Dept. and Grocery Stores 39¢

It's a Big Jump

Yes, it's a big jump from washing diapers the old way and using Rock-A-Bye Diaper Wash.

The Rock-A-Bye way is so easy .... just dip, swish, rinse ... and there you are. Diapers come clean, sweet and white in Rock-A-Bye Diaper Wash.

And there are more surprises in the Rock-A-Bye line .... fast Bottle Wash for example, makes short work of washing Baby's nursing bottles. And don't forget Rock-A-Bye Baby Soap for tender baby skin.

It's for Baby
Buy Rock-A-Bye

At all Drug, Dept. and Grocery Stores 39¢

Rock-A-Bye Baby products were going to push Johnson & Johnson off the shelves. They didn't. Like many post-war product introductions, Rock-A-Bye went bye-bye. Even today, two out of three new product introductions are failures. Forgive the corny headline, I was but a youth (and the artist) at the time.

When you judge advertising, one thing to be considered - ruefully perhaps - is that 90 per cent of consumers are *not* like you.

The Martini Illusion

It seems to be a trait of human nature to believe that God made everyone in your own image. A bibulous example is the Martini Illusion: if you are a typical literate, educated person, it is likely that you regard the martini as a popular drink, perhaps so popular it is a little lowbrow. Almost everybody I know in the advertising business drinks martinis. A lot of people in the liquor business think everybody drinks martinis. When I made the advertising for Gilbey's gin, we had interviewers ask people what they really drink. Here is what we found: only half the population drank gin at all. Only *four per cent* of them drank martinis. That's one in twenty-five, *four* in a hundred.

Recently I asked a Seagram executive whether my information is still valid; after all, in the succeeding years people could have become more suave and sophisticated, leading to higher absorption of martinis. Sure enough, things *have* changed. Nowadays in North America only *ten per cent* of people are gin drinkers and the number is shrinking. And today only *one* person in a hundred drinks martinis even though many of us who supposedly know the consumer continue to live in the false impression that the martini is a universal favourite.

The Martini Illusion illustrates how each of us lives in an island of experience that very often is *not* a microcosm of the nation's tastes. Even my example may be outdated as white wine and club soda replace the martini as the preprandial tranquilizer.

The illusion that one and one's friends represent a cross-section of the population is strong among the people who create advertising. It is astonishing how soon a copywriter who has grown up on hamburger, Kraft Dinner, and Coke forgets, and imagines that everyone dines on Boeuf à la Bourgignonne, Pasta alla oleo, and a charming little Chianti or burgundy. They usually make larger salaries than their relatives ever thought them capable of. If you are to understand the forces that shape advertising, you should recognize that the climate in which it grows is not necessarily the same as yours.

Women Dominate Consumer Buying

The important fact to bear in mind if you are to understand advertising is this: *Women are the purchasing agents for their families. Women buy over 80 per cent of advertised products.* This role will, if anything, increase in your lifetime. The family unit, as a buying force, while showing some turnover in personnel, will persist as long as we can see into the future. And most of the evidence is that women will make the buying decisions.

These premises are not what you would deduce from watching TV or reading the newspapers or magazines. But the facts are there in your government's statistics. Will the family survive, and the woman persist as its economic decision-maker? Read on.

1. *Nearly all grown-up women are married.* Among women over the age of twenty, about seven out of ten are married. One in ten is a widow. Less than two out of ten (15 per cent, if you wish) are single. There are not many widowers. About four widows survive for every bereaved male; women live longer than men for some reason or other.*

Marriage, apparently, is not all that bad. More women are getting

---

* Statistics Canada, 1981.

divorces but, while marriage among women in their twenties is being delayed, the fastest growing marriage category is among divorcées.* And my twice-married friends claim that "the divorce rate among second marriages is lower than among first marriages." There may be a certain amount of facing reality here as second wives and husbands are becoming a little long in the tooth for further conquests.

2. *Women are marrying at about the same rate as ever*. Half of the single women who get married in Canada are under twenty-three years of age.** If you find this hard to believe it is probably because there is a distinct growth in the number of women who are holding off marriage until they are over twenty-five - around 5 per cent.† It is very likely that these women who hold off marriage are in higher proportion among our friends.

Three out of ten marriages in Canada will end in divorce (it is five out of ten in the U.S.). Half the people who divorce have no children. Women ask for about twice as many of the divorces as men. Most marriages that end in divorce last from five to ten years. Two out of three marriages that start out with a bride under age twenty end in divorce.†† This sounds alarming until you realize that nearly half the women who get divorced remarry, keeping the family unit going, and that the divorce rate seems to be leveling off in Canada.

It takes both yin and yang to make a marriage. The most yang of media, *Playboy*, had researchers ask nearly 2,000 men, eighteen to forty-nine, their attitudes about family, sex, politics. Three out of four said sexual fidelity was very important for a successful marriage and that "having another person to share one's life" was very important. Eighty per cent said family life was a very important thing in life, and, in fact, most of them said it is "the most important." Marriage may be weak in the flesh but the will is there.

3. *The family seems to be surviving and it has more money to spend*. Woods Gordon, money consultants, says that "The family is still the major purchasing unit . . . ." North American families have more *real* buying power than ever before in history. Working women are helping fatten the family budgets. Added to this, the Conference Board of Canada predicts that the number of family households will increase at

---

* *Ibid.*

** Conference Board of Canada, *Handbook of Canadian Consumer Markets*, 2nd ed., 1982.

† Statistics Canada, *Quarterly Catalogue*, October-December, 1982.

†† *Vital Statistics*, vol. II, 1979.

least until the year 2001.* Even then the number of people getting together to form households will drop only to the 1951-61 rate. About one home in ten is a single-parent family.** These parents are almost always women - divorced, deserted, with a tiny fraction never married (about 33,000 out of 5 million families in Canada).†

Family spending reaches its peak when the woman is between the ages of thirty and thirty-five. That's when you buy all that baby food, those endless booties, boots, buggies, and bikes, Jello, Froot Loops, TV sets, dental braces, Sugar Corn Pops, Tide, Duz, Fab, and Mr. Clean, glad rags, Glad bags, station wagons, McDonald's and Harvey's burgers, frozen cakes, pies, pizzas, potatoes, and acetylsalicylic acid.

There is some concern that the present diffidence about child-bearing among certain women and men may eliminate the family. Our birth rate, after all, is dropping below the level at which our population will naturally reproduce itself. Families are slowly growing smaller. Also, with more children (one in ten) growing up with a non-family background, they may carry on the habit in their own lives. Then again, they could be more attracted to the security of family life. Perhaps, too, in a generation or two, people who do not have a taste for reproducing themselves will be bred out of the stock by natural selection. The family unit, through practical need, human affection, and five million years of experiment, seems likely to continue.

4. *There are 5.5 million children under age fifteen in Canada.* The purchasing agents for the home (mothers perhaps?) make most of the choices for this vociferous, insistent, and increasingly self-conscious group. Children are intensely aware of what brands of shoes and clothes others wear at school, and they make life hell for the parent who is not sensitive to what will keep a child from feeling like a leper. They want to look older - and *slim*. If you want to understand McDonald's advertising, remember, when the family eats out the children choose where they will eat four out of ten times. As long as there are children in our society, women will make the buying decisions most of the time - as often as not buying to fend off powerful pressure from the most powerful pressure group of all.††

5. *The number of "one-person households," as the statisticians call them, has grown from around 10 per cent to over 15 per cent in the*

---

* Conference Board of Canada, *Consumer Markets*, 1982.

** *Census of Canada*, 1981.

† Conference Board of Canada, *Consumer Markets*, 1982.

†† Statistics Canada, *Quarterly Catalogue*, October-December, 1982.

past ten years. This may be a temporary state caused (a) by delayed marriages and (b) by the population bulge that filled schools to bursting from the sixties into the seventies. The singles phenomenon may be the wave rolling through.

Where in the statistics do we find men and women who are simply living together? There is, in the Canadian statistics, a category called "non-family households, two or more persons." They account for about one household in twenty.* And if you accept the estimate that 10 per cent of men, at least, are homosexual, the two-person household number is further out of kilter. In the U.S. the number of women aged thirty to thirty-four who are unmarried is increasing, but so is the number of people living together in "consensual unions," or non-official marriages.**

Perhaps there has *always* been a certain proportion of people living together, only today we talk about it more. It's no longer sinful to live in sin. Or it may be that the growth of "one-person households" does not take into account the number of double beds.

I have been puzzled by the overwhelming illusion that marriage and the family are doomed, even though a half hour with the statistics tables demonstrates otherwise. I can only attribute the illusion to the tendency of journalists to magnify small trends into avalanches. There is the likelihood that journalists themselves are restless people who are well-educated and well-to-do, travel a lot, meet a great variety of stimulating folk, and are possibly above average in intelligence; and they may not themselves have stable marriages. In the magic mirror of their own experience they see the state of the nation. (I am told that one Canadian women's magazine reflects the latest status of its editor in its articles and features on love and marriage.)

I have no statistics to support my conjecture about journalistic tendencies. But look what reporters and headline writers can do with statistics: "Report says divorce rate is up and fewer people are marrying" (Toronto *Globe and Mail*). The text speaks of a "jump" of 8 per cent in the rate of divorce per 100,000. This means that in all of Canada there were *less than a thousand* more divorces than the year before. Perhaps the spate of journalism about single living, double living, serial monogamy, boring marriages, and unfulfilled lives is caused by the number of journalists living alone, living with lovers permanently or serially, suffering (or causing) boring marriages, and fulfilling their lives through journalism.

It seems, from the statistics, that nearly everybody ends up married

---

* *Census of Canada*, 1981.

** *Scientific American*, August, 1983.

or living fairly permanently with someone eventually. And although there are more males pushing shopping carts these days, the woman most often will be the buyer for whomever depends on her - husband, children, lover(s).

6. *More than five out of ten Canadian women work.* Among married women less than half have permanent jobs.* A higher proportion of younger married women under twenty years old have jobs, presumably to help the miserable salaries their too-young husbands earn. (And all this effort to pave the way to those divorces at age thirty-five!)

Having children has little effect on whether a woman chooses to work or not. These working women like to work. In a U.S. study, reported in the *Harvard Business Review*, a thousand working women were asked whether they would stay at home if they could make the same money. Six out of ten said they would prefer to work. A majority of women college graduates go to work. However, less than one in ten working women consider their job "a career." This ambitious group may be increasing. Most of the women studied did not really work for money. Only one in five said income is the main reason for working. Most say it is "an interest outside the home," for "companionship," or because "friends are working." Although the world economy has tightened and more women will be working to supplement the family budget, they will doubtless continue to enjoy working.

Working does little to alter the woman's role as purchasing agent for the family unit, except that the working woman has more to spend and has less time for diversion. Many women like to use the money they earn to buy clothes for themselves, cosmetics, and personal luxuries - a new freedom. They are able to acquire some of the things that make life more pleasant around the home - the dishwasher, the extra TV set, the second car.

The best route for a woman aiming at the executive suite is through sales, marketing, or advertising. Two U.S. studies found that the national average of women executives was 1 per cent. But in marketing and advertising 9 per cent of executives working on the top 500 big-spending brands are women. On June 18, 1983, Ogilvy & Mather, New York, announced fourteen new vice-presidents. Eight were women.

7. *In the United States and Canada, about half the population, female and male, has no more than an elementary education.* One of every two people who respond to advertising may have difficulty reading without moving their lips. Sophisticated humour leaves them baffled. Clever plays on words confuse them.

---

* Statistics Canada, 1981.

26

About 5 per cent of people in Canada over the age of fifteen have graduated from university.* Women continue to shy away from courses in engineering and forestry and lean toward subjects like education, nursing, languages, the humanities. More women are beginning to enter the fields of commerce and business administration, subjects that would arm them for careers in business and advertising, but there are still about three times as many male graduates in these disciplines. It is a good direction for women to follow. In looking at the women MBA graduates of 1973, *Fortune* magazine ten years later found that thirty-three out of thirty-four were working, married, and had a median salary of $57,000. Fourteen were mothers.

More women get degrees in medicine than in commerce and business administration. The number of women becoming systems analysts and computer programmers has increased six-fold in the past ten years. But at last count the number was still only 17,000.

8. *The back-to-the-land craving is another chimera existing largely in newspaper type and the phosphor on your TV screen.* In Canada, nine out of ten Canadians live in towns of 10,000 or more people. Seven out of ten Canadians live in cities of 100,000 or more.** When you get right down to it, a quarter of all Canadians live in *just three cities.* Some frontier image. For every rugged individualist who hews wood and pumps water there are a thousand who prefer the thermostat. A few women may be earth mothers delving in potato patches, growing chives and thyme, and cosseting the milche cow. But the evidence is that most women prefer the clatter of the shopping cart and the camaraderie of the check-out line.

9. Whenever you find yourself troubled by the North American woman's lack of outlets for creative gratification, consider this: *the average North American woman watches over three and a half hours of TV every day.* In the evenings, she is usually accompanied by the average North American man. When do working women find time to *work?* Remember, if that is the average, then about half the women watch *more* than that.

"Prime time," the hours when most people are basking in the glow of *Bob Newhart* and *The Jeffersons,* is from 8 p.m. to 11 p.m. Advertisers pay high prices for these three high-audience hours. But there are millions of people watching earlier and later. Who can deny the strength of the news, at whatever hour? The afternoon soap operas have a possible audience of the 50 per cent of women who do not work and the other 25 per cent who work part-time. Probably the only thing

---

* Conference Board of Canada, *Consumer Markets,* 1982.
** *Ibid.*

that keeps women from spending more time watching TV is that Saturday and Sunday afternoons are full of beer and sports. (I've often thought, since many homes now have two television sets, a clever programmer would schedule some female-appeal shows for women to watch to escape the football games and the Cowgirls.) Every day a typical woman is exposed to about a hundred advertising messages on TV alone. Then there's breakfast radio, car radio, and the newspapers. And *Family Circle, Reader's Digest, Chatelaine, Flare,* and *Canadian Geographic Journal* - hundreds more advertising messages.

Some of the figures and statistics about the family, education, and working women that I have placed before you may surprise you. I know that they will be news to a great many marketers and advertisers who also have been deluded by what they learn from the media. (The marketers and advertisers, too, are intelligent, bored, and frequently away from hearth and home or divorced.) The figures are all there in Canada's census information, in books and computer tapes for you to prowl through yourself.

Most advertising is created to influence women. As nearly as I can describe them, the women in this chapter are the women who, by their acceptance or rejection, shape Canada's and North America's advertising.

CHAPTER 3

The Anatomy of an Advertising Agency

At cocktail parties and soirées I am occasionally asked, "What does an advertising agency *do?*" If you are to understand how advertising is shaped, it may be helpful for you to have a rough idea of the inner workings of an advertising agency.

Long ago, advertising agencies started out as agents who sold advertising space. Publications paid these agents a commission. Eventually, probably to gain a competitive edge, the agents helped advertising customers to compose their messages. To this day the essential work of an advertising agency is buying advertising space in publications (and time in TV and radio) and helping advertisers create effective messages. Advertising agencies are still paid, not by the clients but by the newspapers, magazines, and broadcasters. The rate is 15 per cent of the cost of time or space used.

As advertising grew and proved effective, spending got bigger and, of course, the 15 per cent grew larger and more attractive. To compete, agencies added services. Today, an advertising agency may have as many as ten departments and many satellite services. A large agency will have from 100 to 2,000 people doing everything from measuring advertisements to writing music, cajoling movie stars, studying computer printouts, taste-testing recipes, and drawing birthday cards for the client's wife. It's like "You Can't Take It With You," only you can get fired.

The Clients

To understand how many advertising agencies have taken the shape they have, you must know roughly how the companies that manufacture and sell the products are organized. Companies are as different as families. Some are run dictatorially, others by consensus. Some have virtually a civil service way of operating, others are nearly guerrilla warriors.

Today, few of the large companies that sell to consumers are managed by one person, an owner, president, entrepreneur. Not too many years ago, Noxzema was single-handedly launched in Canada and made into a big force in skincare by Marvin Shaw, a powerful salesman and inspirational company head. George Washington Hill, supposed model for the tyrannical boss in *The Hucksters*, dominated the advertising for the American Tobacco Company and for Lucky Strike. Fred McBrian ran Bristol-Myers single-handedly in the early sixties. Goodyear Tire, General Foods, Borden, Campbell, Rowntree, Lipton, Guaranty Trust, London Life Insurance, Rothman, Seagram, Gilbey, Schweppes were all run - sales, marketing, and advertising - by strong individuals in Canada during the fifties and into the sixties. I sold campaigns to all of them.

But as marketing and advertising grew complex, and as many of the old dogs retired to spend their fortunes, the shape of marketing organizations changed. The top 100 businesses in Canada have sales ranging from $700 million (Kraft) to $12 billion (Canadian Pacific). Many of the top companies - oil and gas producers, forest products and heavy machinery manufacturers, mining - do not sell directly to consumers. But as the recession years of 1982-83 have reminded us, all depend in the end on consumer demand. Among the top 100 in sales are four supermarket food chains. Two meatpackers are larger in sales than any of the conventional packaged goods companies. Procter & Gamble ranks 87th in dollar sales. It is the largest in consumer advertising spending. Nabisco is 94th in sales, 7th in advertising. (Kodak, McCain, Lever Bros., Campbell, and Kellogg are all among the top 100 advertising spenders in Canada but are not among the top 100 in sales.)

Most companies that spend large advertising dollars are packaged goods companies or other outfits who have built their marketing divisions in imitation of packaged goods companies. Packaged goods companies, led by Procter & Gamble, have been successful in organizing their troops to handle the almost unmanageable business of telling people about their many products.

Thousands of businesses do *not* work in the way I am about to describe. While I admire the checks and balances of the giants, I usually find it greater fun to work with more entrepreneurial minds. What

I have learned from the Goliaths, I can put at the service of the Davids.

Client Structures and Agency Organization

Today, a company that sells detergents or baby foods or cleansing creams has a hierarchy of princes and heirs apparent. Many of them are MBAs, impatiently waiting for the old guard to perish. Let us begin with the top person, the *president* or the *chief executive officer*. Under him (it is still almost always a man) come the main divisions of the company: (1) the group that makes the product, called *manufacturing*; (2) the group that sells the product, which used to be called the sales department* and is now the *marketing department*; (3) a group that invents new products or services and improves the old, known as *research and development*; and (4) a group that takes in and pays out the money, the *finance department*.

Marketing

The marketing department tells the advertising agency what the company has to sell and how much. Marketing departments are generally divided up by products. Even if they sell services, like credit cards or term insurance, they are usually called products. Under the marketing director you will find overseers of groups of products, three different detergents, say, or margarines, or cake mixes, or shampoos and other beauty aids. Then comes the "brand man" (I think they have recently slid into the less sexual "brand *manager*"), usually responsible for the life and prosperity of one brand, like Jello or Modess. And of course there are assistants, juniors. There are continuing experiments at insinuating women into these tiered structures; they remain, thus far, predominantly male.

All of these strata in the client's company are working to sell the product to you, the consumer. You help make up the pages in their consumer usage studies. How much detergent do you use per wash? Do you measure it out with a cup or just guess? Do you *plan* to buy a frozen cheesecake or buy it on impulse? Or both? And if both, how often for each? Do you worry about "heavy" days? If you are a university graduate, are you more or less inclined to use vodka? Stick shift automobiles? Margarine? Why do you hate milk?

A lot of the work done by the lower strata of the marketing department is calculation and projection of what your demand will be for a

---

* The sales department/marketing department's job is to persuade storekeepers to stock the product. This involves the travelling salesman, without whom vaudeville humour would have died years sooner. Despite computerization of ordering, inventory control, and sophisticated communications, there seem to be more salesmen than ever.

product or service. This is work that computers can do faster and unemotionally. Eventually, many of the layers in marketing departments will be replaced by miniature chips and transistors that never tire, don't have office affairs, and don't make the agency account executive buy three-martini lunches.

Marketing people have to persuade you to buy their brands. Their jobs depend on it. They have many ways to make their products attractive to you: packaging, size, flavour, convenience, price - and advertising. It is usually through the marketing groups that advertising agencies deal with clients. In the simple days of yore, one person at the agency talked to one person at the client's place. As often as not, the agency talked to the president or his advertising manager. As layer was added to layer in the client's marketing department, the agency has had to add layers to match. You can't have a client vice-president being served by a mere account supervisor. And client juniors feel uncomfortable talking to mature, experienced advertising people. The result is that, layer by layer, advertising agencies have built mirror images of marketing departments. Today it would take only the addition of a packaging line and a few travellers to turn some agencies into complete soap companies.

A large amount of advertising planning and creation starts at the wet-eared bottom layers of account people and brand people. It then works its way up, running a gauntlet of vetoes until it reaches the top. A commercial or an advertisement is often a pale, wan shadow of itself after it has been doctored to suit the tastes of various levels and fiddled with to outguess the tastes of the bosses at the next level. Getting a new idea through to the top decision-maker is like trying to pour water through the wrong end of a funnel. Sigurd Larmon, one-time head of Young & Rubicam, said, as I recall it, "If you want someone to say 'Yes,' you have to go to the top. Everyone else is only able to say 'No.'"

It has always amused me that the promotion of many products for women is dominated so completely by men. At this very moment (or tomorrow morning at the latest) entire boardrooms of men - grey-haired president, vibrant marketing men, pert young brand men, kinetic account executives, omniscient creative directors - are probably sitting around the mahogany looking at computer-generated graphs and figures, seeking prescience about the mysterious behaviour of the North American woman: Which instant food or eating-out place will she flit toward next? Which soup or frozen pizza, jelly powder or dog food, diet drink or basted turkey will capture her attention? And rarely a woman in sight to suggest answers to these trenchant questions. Companies who simply made products and offered them for sale in stores have developed into *mille-feuilles* of stratified organizations. They often become so complex it takes entire armies of management consultants to untangle the mess in times when overweight threatens financial health.

Just as many manufacturers have expanded into complex organisms, so have their agencies. Advertising agencies are roughly departmentalized to bring a little order out of chaos. Here is a brutally simplified description of what must be the most complex sub-society outside a university faculty.

The Agency Salespeople

Account Services. The salespeople for the advertising agency are called "account executives." In fiction and on television (i.e., *Bewitched* reruns) account executives are the heroes, the Hairbreadth Harrys who conjure up slogans at the last minute and save the account. In real life, a good account executive is a practical business person, probably more like a lawyer than anything more flamboyant.

An advertising agency is an assembly of talents like a symphony orchestra. A good account executive is like a good orchestra leader who coaxes the best performance from all the talents. A successful account executive should be an adroit handler of people, both in the agency and in the client's office, a double-edged salesman. I still feel compelled to use the term "salesman" here rather than "sales*person*" to describe this historic activity. Women are entering the job, but it is men who have created the stereotype. *Death of a Salesperson* would not make a great play title. An increasing number of women are emerging as account executives, as they have done in such other areas of selling as real estate and used cars.

If you want to imagine the atmosphere of the advertising agency, especially the New York variety, I find that the films *Network* and *Kramer vs. Kramer* give a reasonably accurate picture of the working climate of the industry. The account executive world bristles with macho, war-like language: advertising "campaigns," "blitzes," "launching attacks against" markets, market "penetration," "target" markets, "shotgun approach," as if marketers were entering supermarkets with Tommy guns to do battle with the Amazons. I have suggested to marketers that they will succeed better if they make love, not war.

Women are entering advertising and marketing in larger numbers as more of them are processed through business schools. The Master of Business Administration degree gives you a mystique comparable with that of a medical degree. So sacred were MBAs in the seventies that agencies and manufacturers snapped them up like hotcakes. Too hot, it turned out at times: these imagos emerged from pupal state at the University of Western Ontario or the Harvard Business School as fully formed presidents or chief executive officers. Then, like the Prince of Wales, they had to futz around in demeaning middle-level jobs.

The department that harbours account executives is usually called "Account Services." The account executive, for all the exalted sound of the name, is the low creature on the totem pole in the department, unless the agency is so insensitive to modern nomenclature as to have *assistant* account executives. In big agencies there are usually three or four levels of account executives: manager of account services (a vice-president* or, as numbers proliferate, a *senior* vice-president); account managers, who handle groups of accounts and are inevitably vice-presidents; account supervisors; and the account executive. Today - with only the most bizarre exceptions, like the nephew of the client's treasurer - *all* of these levels will be university-educated.

Account people used to think of themselves as sellers. Today many prefer to think of themselves as *marketing* people who understand their clients' vexations as clearly as do the clients themselves. Nevertheless, the *prime* reason for understanding the clients' business is to be able to sell advertising campaigns to the clients. "Sell" is a crass word to describe the subtle communication, the massaging of egos, the ruminant digestion of staggering columns of boring figures, the inspired interpretation of research questions, and the countless other trivia that comprise an account executive's expertise. But it *is* selling.

It may seem odd that an advertising agency needs four levels of university graduates to carry television commercials and rough sketches of advertisements and posters over to the client. Indeed, sometimes the client comes to the agency. Account people, men and women, are today called "suits," which is perhaps some measure of their substance.**

The account executives have the toughest job in the agency, blamed by agency people when the client rejects their work, first on the client carpet when sales falter. Account people tend to be strong personalities, very logical thinkers, convergent thinkers who arrive at answers step by step, unlike creative people, who sometimes leap to a conclusion more by intuition than logic. These personality differences cause the toughest people problems in advertising agencies. A famous creative person, Roy Whittier, creative director of Young & Rubicam, whimsically describing the expendibility of most ad agency depart-

---

* Fred Allen wrote all his radio shows himself - weekly - a herculean creative job. He was constantly in conflict with advertising agencies. He said something like this: "When an advertising vice-president comes to work in the morning, he finds a molehill on his desk. It is his job, before he goes home that night, to make a mountain out of it."

** Like the armoured futuristic soldiers in *Barbarella* that, when blown apart, proved to contain nothing.

ments, said, "And the account executives, do we need them? A good messenger service could do the job faster and cheaper."

Deciding Where the Advertising Should Appear

Media Department. This is the department that decides where you will see or hear the advertising messages, whether the medium will be TV, newspapers, radio, magazines, billboards, or skywriting. (The plural, *media*, is often improperly used by advertising people in a singular sense: "Television is a good media.")

A friend of mine was trying to tell her European grandmother what she did in the media department. "I buy space and time," she explained. "Yoi. Who do you think you are - God?"

Shop Talk

Many people think business publications talk only about machinery. Not so. There is a Maclean Hunter publication just for doctors, another for jewellers, one for hotel-keepers, another for forestry engineers. In their own shop talk, we bring news to such diverse specialists as aviators, salespeople, teachers, oil drillers, fashion photographers, secretaries, builders, retailers. While Maclean Hunter has shown strong growth in electronic media, we remain the major, and sometimes the only, source of relevant information for people in most businesses and professions across Canada. We are proud of our role in helping Canada to be one of the most prosperous nations on earth.

Only the editor of a small-town weekly newspaper could know his audience as well as, say, the editor of Marketing magazine knows his marketing and advertising community.

And when you write to hold the interest of special groups like engineers, truck fleet owners, restaurateurs, pharmacists, fashion designers, supermarket operators, mechanics and other professionals it takes expert knowledge, experience and a keen interest in the field.

Maclean Hunter is fortunate in the calibre of writing and editing in

its business publications. To name but four of the 75 in Canada: one of the oldest, Hardware Merchandising, has been serving that market for more than 80 years. Canadian Grocer was established in 1887. Aerospace Canada is circulated in 160 countries and Canadian Datasystems, like most Maclean Hunter business publications, is the leading publication in its field.

Advertisers who want to talk to specialists in their own language know that their messages are often as intensively read in these authoritative publications as is the

editorial content. Often a Maclean Hunter publication is the only regular source of Canadian information on a profession or market.

Ideas and services are our major products. They can only be as good as the people who create them.

Maclean Hunter is 99% Canadian owned and aggressively proud of it. We make it possible for many of our people to own stock and more than two thirds do so. There is a certain extra involvement when one has a piece of the action.

 Maclean Hunter

The illustration on the reverse page is from the cover of **Canadian Photography**, a publication that puts professional photographers and photographic dealers in the picture on technology and technique. This is but one of 75 business and professional publications, expertly written and edited by Maclean Hunter people.

Although my reputation has been built largely upon products you buy in grocery stores, I have, of late, become known for what is called "advocacy" advertising. This message for Maclean Hunter is one of a series that speaks essentially to business people, government people, advertisers, and investors about the company. The woman's face was used on the cover of one of their many publications, Canadian Photographer. *You may argue that a female face is inappropriate for selling a male-oriented publication. However, many of the people who select media for advertising purposes are women, and, according to my observations, would be stopped by a woman's picture.*

The media department is largely manned by women. I don't know for sure why this is. George Murray, the machine who has headed Ogilvy & Mather's media department in Canada for twenty-two years, has selected his people during all that time using aptitude tests. The result has been a media department dominated by clever young women. This influence has been felt in many, if not most, media departments in Canada, for graduates from his tough training move on to run the departments in other agencies while George continues to discover new generations of efficiency. Maybe women are better than men at finicky work with figures. Maybe you can buy more mathematical IQ per dollar. Whatever the reason, women predominate in media departments.

You might believe that choosing the medium for the message is easy. And it is. Today, in addition to you consumers being catalogued by marketing people, you also contribute - for the use of media folk - to all the little magnetic blips on computer tapes telling what kind of people read newspapers, watch soap operas, read *Reader's Digest, Chatelaine, Homemaker's,* or *Canadian Living.* All I have to know is what kind of people I want to reach and how often; the computer chatters out the answers. I am selling, say, a margarine with little cholesterol problem. I decide my best prospects will be university graduates, married, over thirty-five, living mostly in cities over 50,000. This is duck soup for the media people and the computer. They tell the machine these criteria and it immediately types out a list of media for me.

The real art in choosing media is in deciding in the first place who *are* the prospects for your advertising. When we were selling expensive condominium suites (1984 prices would be $250,000 to $1,000,000), we chose one newspaper that reached the business, social, and political cream in the city. Unlike most advertisers who hope to appear grand, we used small advertisements, about a sixth of the page, more like Tiffany's than Macy's. Each advertisement described a feature of the suite, such as sound-proofing, marble bathroom sink, or whatever. And each advertisement featured the prices of the suites, usually starting with the *highest* price (the real estate sales people winced) and working down. The audience for these messages included, of course, the people who intended to buy. But *the most important audience was the friends, the relatives, the rivals, and the competitors of the people who would buy.* And we sold the condominiums.

Even with the help of computers, selecting media is often a creative art. Popular taste and habits shift and turn, frequently in surprising ways as our society evolves. The media person is continuously dealing with amazing information. In Canada, particularly, the public is defying fellow-Canadian Marshall McLuhan and is turning more than ever to the written word. Bookstores multiply. Newspapers grow fat. Magazines thrive as never before. Where once magazines had to have nationwide appeal to survive, they now thrive in single cities: all major Canadian cities now support local magazines. Canada has created another phenomenon not widespread in the States, the free magazine. These magazines are delivered at no cost to the homes of selected people, usually chosen because they live in higher-income areas. Certain advertisers like this because they can talk directly to the people who have money to spend on such up-scale products as frozen desserts, imported cars, fine wines, computers, and smoked meats.

Women between the ages of twenty-five and forty-nine have several favourite magazines: *Chatelaine*, *Reader's Digest*, *Maclean's*, and *Canadian Living*. *TV Guide* and *TV Times* are equally success-ful - good advertising media, for people truly do look at them many times a week. Many magazines claim they stay around and are picked up many times but few with the justification of the TV magazines.

Television is gigantic in its influence, but it is weakening. *The Washington Post* had researchers telephone 1,693 people and ask them about TV. They like such shows as *The Waltons*, *The Little House on the Prairie*,* and *Sixty Minutes* and were usually pleased with them. But other shows tended to disappoint them more often than not. Two out of three said that there is too much sex and violence. They found commercials too long and generally in poor taste, but 67 per cent agreed they are a fair price to pay for the entertainment. But most dramatic is the fact that 53 per cent of all those interviewed said they are watching TV less than they did five years ago and more than half of them felt that watching television is the cause of serious problems for children. A third of the people said they would pay to have television without commercials.

Pay-TV will inevitably have some effect on TV viewers but it is unlikely that it will have measurable impact on conventional TV view-ing beyond a couple of percentage points. If it ever reached peak poten-tial saturation, pay-TV would still only be in about 20 per cent of Cana-dian homes. This means that 80 per cent of viewers will be watching commercial TV full-time. And, of course, pay-TV viewers will continue to watch their favourite commercial TV programs. It is doubtful pay-TV can ever match the audience pull of *The Winds of War*, *Roots*, the last episode of *M*A*S*H*, or *The Day After*.

U.S. experience shows that those viewers who subscribe to pay-TV spend *more* time (average 2.5 hours more per week) with their TV sets. There was little drop in viewing of regular commercial programming.

A Gallup poll conducted when pay-TV was first introduced in Canada indicates that 76 per cent of Canadians are not interested in pay-TV. The poll also shows that pay-TV's appeal is strongest with the eighteen to twenty-nine bracket, that men are more interested than women, and

---

* This bucolic craving is curious in nations that are largely city-dwellers. First it was westerns. Now it is rural life. And *Star Wars* augurs a return to the future. Buck Rogers, in 1927, fathered the earlier popular rush into tomorrow as an escape from today. In Ontario, a little back-to-the-land magazine named *Har-rowsmith* has leaped by self-levitation to a strong circulation, a large part of it among advertising executives and other city-bound money-makers hankering for clean air and cow manure.

One of my favourite words - FREE - is in the headline of this ad for energy conservation. I invented the idea of the book and its title, 100 ways to conserve energy and money in the home. The coupon is featured top and centre to encourage people to use it. Each inquiry meant a reader had to clip the coupon, fill it in, buy a stamp, and remember to mail the letter. Two million copies of the book were distributed - a best seller (at the right price). The book made the abstract idea of energy conservation into something concrete.

that English-speaking Canadians are more interested than Francophones.

Mass advertising depends on reaching large numbers of potential customers with a message. Today in Toronto, Montreal, and Vancouver, the audience is divided twenty ways - that is the number of channels available to the average TV cable viewer. With satellite receivers offering sixty channels and video cassette recorders and pay-TV eliminating commercial messages altogether, the thinking in television advertising will alter dramatically in the long run, just as radio advertising changed but did not disappear when television came along.

Television shows come and go as networks try new formulae. In the late seventies *Mork and Mindy* was popular with working women and children between the ages of two and eleven. "Jiggle" shows like *Charlie's Angels*, thought to attract men, did far better with young women and working women. (Is it because those sexy detectives gave evil men their comeuppance that Charlie's Angels were so heavenly to working women?) Young children (between two and eleven) along with working women liked *Three's Company* in the seventies. *Three's Company* is still near the top.

In the eighties, two new formats (not easily duplicated by the movies or pay-TV) have taken hold. First, there are the mini-series like *Shogun* and *The Winds of War*, more gripping by their spectacle than by great writing or acting; they build and hold massive audiences for advertisers. Second, we have seen the rise of the night-time soap operas led by *Dallas* but followed closely by its carbon-copy, *Dynasty* (more popular with working women than *Dallas* at this moment). These macho shows are all from 20 to 50 per cent more popular with adult women than men. *Magnum P.I.* pulls about as many women as men (because, says one media woman, Tom Selleck is such a "hunk"). Afternoon soap operas on TV have a concentrated and avid audience. I could not outline some of the plot lines without blushing. *The Wonderful World of Disney* still pulls large audiences of women, men, and even - though not so powerfully - children.

Finally, and no surprise to anyone, *Hockey Night in Canada* is the best in attracting men and among the worst for women of consuming age. Too bad that men make the purchasing decision only for beer and maybe cars.

The People Who Invent the Advertising

The Creative Department. This is the part of the agency where ads and commercials are made. It is peopled mainly by writers and artists. They are called "creative" people. Largely they are artisans who borrow from the popular culture for ideas that will attract and please the populace. Today, in some agency creative departments, there are writers who can't write and artists who can't draw. They work mostly in television. There are at least as many women writers as men, as well as a growing number of women artists. The people who deal mostly in words are called copywriters (I often suspect because they *copy* one another). The people who deal more in the visual are called art directors. The product of creative departments today is called "the creative" - meaning the advertisement, the poster, or the commercial they have produced. There is a certain illiteracy even in their nomenclature.

The head of the creative department is called the creative director. Once, when I had the job, I received a letter addressed to the "Head of All Creation." I have spent more time in this role than in any other, progenitor or midwife to a thousand campaigns at Young & Rubicam, at Ogilvy & Mather, and at Straiton, Pearson & Martin.

The making of advertising is neither an art nor a science. It is a craft. Even so, the people who make advertising are more creatively inclined than, say, bricklayers. Usually. In the business world, a problem in discussing the creative process is that, of course, everybody is *somewhat* creative. And they all want desperately to believe that they are creative as hell. When somebody says, "Now, I'm not going to write copy, but ..." you can be pretty damn sure they are going to write some copy. There are two jobs everybody in the world can do - their own job and writing copy.

Some psychologists classify about one person in four as *the creative type*. Most of the rest of us are what psychologists call *convergent* thinkers, people who sort of zero in on a clear and logical solution to a problem, remember facts, recognize. The results of convergent thinking are usually not very amazing or risky. This ability - convergent thinking - is what intelligence tests seem to measure.

The other kind of thinking (it appears to happen more often in creative minds) is called *divergent* thinking. J. P. Guilford of the University of Southern California thinks this is the hallmark of the creative thinker. He says creative people are fluent, show originality, see gaps, improvise, use old things in new ways. They are willing to try anything, are less afraid of being wrong than most people. They leap to conclusions, skipping many steps. IQ seems to be separate from creativity, somehow. But creative people with high IQs are probably better creators than creative people with low IQs.

One psychologist says, "Most of the highly creative persons we have seen are not especially well-rounded. They have sharp edges to their personalities, and marked peaks and dips on their personality test profiles." Creative types usually don't like to participate in group activities. Their productivity is low when they do.

A popular idea in business and advertising in the fifties and sixties was "brainstorming," where a bunch of people got in a room together and tossed out ideas - no holds barred - in an attempt to achieve a higher level of idea production. In a test at Yale, brainstorming proved less effective in producing ideas than the same number of individuals working alone. And the ideas of the people working alone proved to be of higher calibre. Brainstorming is a way of forcing non-creative people to be creative.

The creative person is not an organization type. The creative person may not even have the same *values* as the "team." It is Straiton's maxim that garden-variety executives want titles *to show they are over somebody else*. Creative people want titles *to show there is nobody over them*.

The personality traits that make a creative person are usually far different from those that make a good accountant or salesman. Novelists, poets, and painters, for example, produce something that comes out of themselves. It is personal. It is not so much the result of outside pressures. These creative types don't like to be told what to do or how. Dorothy Sayers, F. Scott Fitzgerald, and J. P. Marquand tried advertising copywriting. So have hundreds of others who thought that "writing is writing." These inner-directed people have a rough time in advertising, which is full of rigid rules, sacred cows, and immovable deadlines.

Another kind of creative person is exemplified by mathematicians and scientists. They have the genius to leap great gaps, to observe physical phenomena and create a theory of relativity or an Oedipus complex theory. Not your typical writer of detergent commercials.

The architect shows a further type of creativity that cuts across the others. The architect has to make a building on a certain size lot at a certain cost to serve a certain purpose. Yet, within these rules, the architect can, at times, produce a personal product. In advertising the creative task more closely parallels the architect's.

There is no school to teach young advertising people the realities of creating for practical purposes. Advertising creative types are, almost without exception, self-made. I know many advertising writers who are at the top of their field and who have never gone to a university.

Many agencies treat creative people as temporary phenomena - will o' the wisps. High turnover is thought to be a fact of life in the advertising business. It is, more often, the result of clumsy handling by agency bosses. The final effect is that creative people regard *themselves* as temporary, job-hopping types, sort of disposable. But at Young & Rubicam and at Ogilvy & Mather, creative people worked with me for anything from five to ten years. Our relationships were more successful and lasting than many marriages.

There is a classic summary of the phases of the creative process: assimilation, gestation, inspiration, and evaluation.

1. *Assimilation.* Scientists, poets, inventors, and writers immerse themselves in the problem, *assimilating* facts and figures, literature, gossip, and other grist for the mental mill. Sometimes, it is a life's work, like Marie Curie's or Margaret Mead's. The creative thinker in advertising assimilates the marketing data, the consumer habits, the product formula, the personal experiences, the spouse's opinions, and all the fantastic gestalt of information that goes with a product.

2. *Gestation.* Charles Darwin could chew over his ideas for most of his life. Margaret Atwood can take a year to give birth to a book. In advertising, assimilation is skimmed over under pressure and gestation has a ferocious time limit. There is rarely time to ruminate. I have turned out perhaps ten really trend-setting ideas in my career. Not one of them was on schedule. The gestation period sometimes ran past deadlines; for example, it took me three weeks of mental doodling to develop the much copied Johnson & Johnson "1001 Uses" commercials.

3. *Inspiration.* Nobody can help you here. It is interesting how often great ideas have been conceived when the inventor or author was *not thinking about the problem.* Often it seems to come to people while walking, shaving (putting on makeup), or even sleeping. It is sometimes called the "aha" experience. Archimedes, they say, was soaking idly in his bath when, "Eureka!" he perceived the principle of buoyancy.*

You don't have to force good creative people to think. *You can't stop them.* The creative process is a far cry from the expected pattern for business behaviour. Unless your average organization people can see a writer or artist at the typewriter, *typing*, or at the art board, *drawing*, they feel the work is not being done. A person staring out the window or laughing or doodling may be performing the most important part of the creative job. But it makes most kinds of management pretty nervous.

4. *Evaluation.* Scientists test their theories with experiments. Critics and sales evaluate the work of artists and novelists. Movie attendance is a form of evaluation of a creative product.

One of the great problems of life, especially for some of the less aggressive creative people, is the terrible *Day of Judgement* - the day you present the stuff to the client. No matter how self-confident they say creative people are, or oversold on their ideas, that is ulcer day.

The brand group people have perfected the art of the creative torture. With such bland questions as "Do the words match the picture?" they scare the intuitive copywriter who probably never thought about it. There was one device, used in the days when marriage was sacred, that I called the Wedding Ring Ploy. A group from the soap company (or food or soup or soda pop company) and the apprehensive writer, producer, and account people have screened a commercial showing a woman talking over the fence about how her neighbour's wash is so much whiter. Everyone is congratulating everyone about the impact of the message, the excellent editing, the believable casting, when one brand person says quietly, "Did that woman have a wedding ring?"

Hearts leap. Stomachs sink. The film is rerun. If she *has* a wedding ring, O.K., this person is simply showing care for detail. If she does not have a wedding ring, the commercial might have to be re-shot. A copywriter once mused, "If only Hitler had lived and been made to sit through a Procter & Gamble copy presentation."

There are some ways to avoid the presentation trauma (but not with large, organized brand groups). First, I usually try to remove the need for the big presentation day. If you work properly with other people, it

---

* "Eureka, I have found it!"
  Archimedes cried with hope.
  The principle of buoyancy?
  Nope. The soap.
                                        - J. S. S.

42

is usually possible to *bring them along with your thinking.* "Spring no surprises." Discussion often takes the rough edges off an idea.

Sometimes our clients see ideas in almost doodle form. Then we *test* the ideas with research. The ideas we test are usually in a rough, simple form - descriptive sentences, sketchy ads, or home-movie television commercials. They don't have anybody's lifeblood in them. Everyone can be pretty sanguine about the results. A client can say, "Ha ha, so they don't think it's important that we've been making stoves since 1887." The *consumer* makes the judgement. The sting is far less when the judgement is made by an objective test. It's easier for the creative person to say, "Well, back to the old drawing board." Research has allowed me to make many successful TV commercials and ads we would never have dared to make on instinct alone.

Many great advertising agencies were started by people who had an unusual combination of charisma, business know-how, and creativity. Most of the names that spring to mind are for agencies in the States - David Ogilvy, Raymond Rubicam, Mary Wells, Leo Burnett, Bill Bernbach. Few Canadian agencies are headed by creative people. Warren Brown of Cockfield Brown (recently destroyed) was a print salesman; Jack Maclaren of Maclaren Advertising was a newspaperman and a super-salesman; Gerry Goodis started as an art salesman. Young & Rubicam Canada has been headed by account executives, an art salesman, a university professor. Two Quebec agencies, however, are headed by French-speaking creative women.

Recently a young woman journalist, interviewing me about my creative activity in film-making, asked how I could work at something so uncreative as advertising while making award-winning films. My answer: "Think of me as a carpenter who builds houses in the daytime and makes grandfather clocks at night."

The Agency as a "Clinic" of Advertising Specialists

With all of the history, mistakes, and theory to guide me, you may wonder what sort of agency I have created, starting from scratch. The name of the agency, John Straiton & Partners*, was in my mind for years as a philosophical idea. I used the word "Partners" to express an organization philosophy that contrasted with the usual military, pyramidal structure many sixties' agencies had developed. My concept of an advertising agency is as an assemblage of talents - writers,

---

* I have since changed the name to include those of my two earliest partners. We now call our enterprise Straiton, Pearson & Martin, but the philosophy remains the same.

artists, media and research experts, sales people - all important specialists, banded together for mutual gain. It is like a medical clinic where various specialists are gathered to give you a high level of diagnosis and treatment. Rather than a military pyramid, with creative people reporting to account people, media people reporting to research people or vice versa, I visualize a phalanx of high-quality professionals, all partners in an advertising "clinic."

It is my dream to produce the highest calibre of work for a select group of intelligent advertisers. I hope to develop our reputation to the point that clients appreciate our professional expertise and we work together in mutual respect. And I hope that where this does not exist, we divorce. Some advertisers submit their agencies to a review of performance every few months. On my first such servant's line-up at General Foods, as president of Ogilvy & Mather, I took along a list of things I thought they should do to improve their performance as a client. I think they found it refreshing and helpful. But the account people were alarmed and I was never asked to attend one of these performances again. Agency appraisals are probably useful and necessary to companies with several agencies, or to those so large that intimate relationships are impossible and lines of command are long.

How Big Should an Advertising Agency Be?

Usually in a healthy client/agency relationship there are good vibes between a few key people from the client company and two or three people in the agency. Inevitably, the agency people are a creative/account service mix. However large or small the agency, the number of people keenly interested in the account is pretty well a constant. This nucleus of active minds is what clients want applied to their business. The chances of this sort of productive relationship diminishes as turnover of agency people accelerates.

One of the heaviest crosses borne by the management of large agencies is their enslavement to the whims and caprices of their creative people. Many of these creative people are interested only in creating television commercials and refuse to be bothered with newspaper or magazine advertising. Some creative people even refuse to work on products that don't excite them, such as detergents, sanitary napkins, or products whose story or budget is not right for television. To many of these creative people, advertising is more a paid ego trip than a profession. Their object, all too often, is to collect samples of clever advertising that they can use to sell their talents to the next agency creative director.

Turnover in creative people in agencies is pandemic. Turnover in account people is a parallel problem, as agencies buy one another's trained people. Agencies are like the clouds on the leeward side of a mountain peak ... somehow keeping their constant shapes while water droplets go in one end and out the other.

I have told advertisers, "If you feel in your heart that a client-agency marriage should involve some constancy, especially in creative and account service, then the state of much of our industry should alarm you. For some very large advertisers, where institutions and systems are really more important than chemistry, turnover is not a serious problem. For them, one big agency is about as good as another. But if your company is not in the top 100 advertisers (or even if it is), quality, creativity, and dedication may mean more to you. The cutting edge of your marketing may be sharpened by your advertising. How do you find dedication, stability, drive, aggressiveness all in one place? Try looking at agencies in which the key people who work on your account own a piece of the agency action."

I have had it pointed out to me that "an advertising agency is a service business." There are degrees of service that range all the way from pimping to brain surgery. I prefer to see our services as being closer to the brain surgeon end of the spectrum.

CHAPTER 4

Talking with Consumers

I have never had great self-confidence. I do not have that inner strength of rightness that supports many advertising and business careers. For these reasons I have always turned to research to support my statements. When I boldly state that "Women prefer to look at pictures of women and men prefer pictures of men," you are not hearing my opinion but the statement of a principle discovered through studies of how people look at advertising.

Many advertising agencies and marketers base *some* of their decisions on the public's needs and reactions to products and advertising. They tend, however, to leave a great many decisions to conventional wisdom, or to gut feeling.

Because of my personal timidity, I support every decision, as far as possible, on what we can learn from the consumer. The result, over the years, has been an approach to advertising dictated by consumers. My advertising is almost always based on consumer reactions rather than personal intuition and creative inspiration. When I or my partners *do* have a hunch, my first reaction is to try it out on the people we hope will make the buying decision. And that is, most often, women.

Recently we were studying the spaghetti sauce market. There were four men - two account people and two creative (including me) - participating in this project. All of us were the resident experts on spaghetti sauce in our homes. "Maybe we're onto something here. Maybe men are doing more of the cooking. Maybe some of our advertising should

Mrs. J. D. Royall of Charleston, South Carolina raises fast growing pines as a crop. They compete head on with Canadian forests. While our trees take a lifetime to reach cutting age, some of hers can be harvested in 15 years.

Meet the competition

Research showed that women were not very interested in our messages for the Canadian Pulp and Paper Association. I was delighted to discover this gentle Carolina woman whose business was growing trees on her plantation to compete with Canadian trees. I was able to make an ad that might attract women to read it while alerting Canadians to foreign competition.

Mrs. Royall talks like a gentle Scarlett O'Hara, but she is one tough competitor for the Canadian forest industry.

In ten years of careful management, Mrs. Royall has developed a productive forest on her 200 acres. Plantings of fast growing pine are rapidly approaching the size when they can be harvested to feed U.S. paper mills.

Pulp and paper exports bring in about $1000 a year for each Canadian family, more than any other manufacturing industry.

There are 400,000 plantation owners like Mrs. Royall in the American Tree Farm System.

Competition from other lands is increasing (faster growing forests in warm climates, easy harvesting

To assure future jobs, Canadian governments, along with the forest industry, are increasingly aware of the need for reforestation for future supplies. One Canadian job in ten depends on our forests.

and lower work costs). Thanks to healthier profits, the Canadian pulp and paper industry is able to meet the competition by spending vast sums on new and improved mills and equipment. In 1979, more than one billion dollars was invested to increase efficiency, control energy use and improve the environmental impact of its operations. From coast to coast, companies have announced plans to invest billions more over the next five years to help improve productivity, assure jobs, keep Canada competitive.

Profit that can be invested in growth is important to all Canadians. Pulp and paper products bring in about $1000 a year in export sales for every family in Canada, more than agriculture, mining or petroleum.

Profits invested in modernizing an expanding mills help Canada compete in the tough international market.

For our in-depth publication "Growth", write: Dept. M2 Communications Services, Canadian Pulp and Paper Association, 2300 Sun Life Building, Montreal, Quebec H3B 2X9.

The Pulp and Paper Industry of Canada

be slanted toward men." So, at Toronto's Eaton Centre we asked seventy-five women who had families, "Who makes the spaghetti sauce in your house?" Seventy-four of seventy-five answered, "I do." Only one husband in seventy-five made the spaghetti sauce. If we had depended on our own experience, we might have made a terrible mistake. Research helps avoid succumbing to the Martini Illusion.

Unlike most people in the creative end of advertising I have always been fascinated by the statistics of human behaviour. I majored in psychology at Queen's University. After my first two years in advertising, filled with conflicting and confusing advice, I discovered in a bottom drawer at Young & Rubicam a loose-leaf folder called "Copy Technique Analysis." I felt like someone who had been stumbling around a sandy island pursuing the rumour of buried treasure, who then found a detailed treasure map with an "X" where the gold was hidden.

It is one of the puzzling traits of advertising creative people that the majority of them resist the guidance of research. They somehow prefer not to know whether testimonials make better television commercials. They bitterly resist testing their ads or commercials to discover whether they actually persuade anyone.

When advertising was younger, the pulling power of advertisements was often measured by the number of people who wrote in for the product in a "buried offer." This is an offer of the product buried within the text so that you had to read all the way through to learn about the offer. Different headlines and different text drew better or worse responses. This is an obvious and simple way to find whether advertising works. It is an elementary form of research.

Ideally, the person who is writing an advertisement or a TV commercial would talk to people who might buy the product. There are two problems with this: (1) to talk to a cross-section of people coast to coast, one would need to talk to *hundreds* of people; and (2) writers, like other human beings, believe what they *want* to believe, and would probably listen mostly to the women whose ideas agreed with theirs. (This is known as research "bias," whether shown by a creative person, a research interviewer, or the head of the research department. It is most frequently used by research people to describe the weakness of creative people. I have never heard a research person use "bias" to describe his or her own judgements.) Some advertisers and agencies still require their writers and account people to knock on doors and talk to consumers, which is a good idea: there is nothing like the shock of seeing a real basement laundry room to return a writer to reality.

The research department is an attempt to bring some science to the art of asking people what they like and what arguments are persuasive.

Advertising research has become more and more occult. About the only person who can understand an agency research person is another agency research person. Or a client research person. They talk about "psychographics" in an intimidating manner that turns company presidents to putty. Even silly putty. They talk about "random sampling," "cognitive dissonance," and "semantic differentials" in a manner that makes you feel that to ignore any of these arcane laws would draw a bolt of fire from the heavens.

Some research is so fanatically detailed it is like having a precise topographical map to a thousand-acre swamp. Research tomes have become the present-day demonstration of how many fairies can dance on the head of a pin. It is possible to have a book of 100 pages dealing with the eye movements of 100 people looking at an advertisement, or 500 pages on the moments in life when a cola drink goes well, full of sound and furry interpretation, signifying little. But scraped of all the Babeloney, the research department's job is to find out the things intelligent advertising marketing people, writers, and artists would find out if they could talk objectively with enough people.

The creation of advertising is like tennis. There are instructors, instruction books, scientifically designed racquets, balls, shoes. But in the end it is inevitably intuitive. The advertising research person is dedicated to exact measurement, precision, predictability. The measurements go to degrees of exactness that are usually unusable in the creation of advertising. The research person measures, weighs, and adjusts

48

the way a crack rifle shot measures out gunpowder, balances each bullet, and adjusts the sight with a micrometer screw. Then the rifle is handed to the instinctive copywriter who proceeds to shoot from the hip.

Market Research

Before starting to create advertising we want to know many things about the product (or service) we plan to persuade you to buy. What sort of people will buy this product? How often? What is their income? Do they live in apartments or houses? Do they have oily or dry skin? How often do they use frozen foods? Do they have migraine headaches? Scores of questions like this are answered by market research.

Your living and buying habits are gathered by telephone, by tired interviewers slogging door to door, by diaries filled in by consumers for research companies. All of the information is fed into the computer for the education and guidance of the people who create products and the people who sell and advertise them. The printed version of a market study on a headache remedy, for instance, would be of sufficient weight to compress a paté.

How Do People See the Product or Service?

Today, I fear, a large number of advertising people resist learning about the product. I have discovered some of my best advertising ideas while prowling around the flavours room of a soft drink company or watching women remove the eyes from potatoes for a frozen dinner.

Before long hair made men's hair creams redundant, I advertised a hairdressing gel called Score for Bristol-Myers. I discovered, in talking with one of their scientists during a plant tour, that Score *dissolved in water*. I knew from earlier research for Resdan dandruff preventive that three in four men put water on their hair before applying hair cream. And while advertising another hairdressing, I learned that men did not like the *idea* of putting grease in their hair. Putting it all together, I invented the "Score tap test," the perfect television comparative demonstration. The major competition, Brylcream, was a white dressing for the hair. Our commercials showed a white cream failing to dissolve in the hand under the tap, making a messy smear, while Score, of course, quickly melted into the water, leaving a clean hand. With commercials like this, Score leaped in sales and for a few heady months was neck and neck with Brylcream. (This was about the time *Hair* hit Broadway. Men abandoned hairdressing and eventually the Score tap test went down the drain.)

Positioning the Product or Service

The first step in selling a product is to learn about the needs of the people who will buy it. Edison, well before he made a workable light bulb, became an expert on gas lighting, for that is what he had to beat.

Today, the way you want people to see your product is called its *position*. The word "positioning" is as commonly used in the marketing-advertising culture as, perhaps, "personality" is used in conversation about other people. Procter & Gamble was the first, in the fifties, to put forth the idea of a product's having characteristics that would remain constant throughout its life. They called it the *brand personality*. I remember it well because I was advertising New Blue Cheer at the time. In research, women said cleanliness was more important than whiteness in their choice of a detergent. Innocently, I prepared strong advertising on Cheer's cleaning power, formidable at that time because Cheer used essentially the same formula as another Procter & Gamble product, Tide. My campaign was rejected because P&G had decreed that Cheer's personality would be its ability to produce *whiteness*. *Cleanliness* was reserved for Tide. There is not as yet a detergent with the attribute of *godliness*, although Sunlight and Mr. Clean come close.

Later, in the advertising and marketing culture, the brand *personality* became known as *image*, an idea popularized by David Ogilvy. Then in the sixties, iconoclasts replaced *image* with *position*. Position, or positioning, means many things. A cleansing cream might be positioned as a "medicated product that leaves skin naturally healthy looking," a chemical fruit juice substitute as "a breakfast drink that children and adults can enjoy," a disposable diaper as one that "keeps the baby dry longer."

One of the terrors of positioning is that the client's marketing people and the agency account executives will sometimes decide on the role the product should play *before* consulting consumers. I have seen a deodorant spray with a variable nozzle that would deliver LIGHT, MEDIUM, or HEAVY spray launched on the divine inspiration of client and agency people. They were convinced they knew what the consumer wanted. Consumers ignored the product to death. Evidently women thought they could spray a little more or less and stick to their favourite brand. A simple discussion with a few women would have saved hundreds of thousands of dollars.

The Group Interview

One way of hearing what consumers want and what their attitudes may be is to gather together a few people and talk to them. Some researchers are especially skilled in talking to groups of people and drawing from them ideas that will help in creating an advertising campaign that sells.

Group interviews (sometimes misleadingly called focus groups) are stimulating. They can fool you. If you call in a group from your own acquaintances, or from any source with common ties - a church group, an insurance company, even a single neighbourhood - you risk assembling a group with similar opinions (the Martini Illusion). You can be hoaxed into believing they represent all consumers. Even among randomly chosen strangers, the group interview becomes a social event. The conversation can take a turn that captures everyone's fancy, yet is unrelated to their real beliefs or tastes. Or one charming, forceful, or domineering person can sway the opinion of a group. It requires a clever interviewer to head off one of these runaways. In fact, the *interviewer* may have opinions that, even unconsciously, steer the attitudes of the group.

Perhaps the greatest danger of the group interview is the human tendency to hear what you want to hear from conversation. A writer, an account executive, or a client who is convinced that, say, couturier design is the way to sell pantyhose will seize a single passing reference to fashion design as proof positive that *this* is what all women crave.

For these reasons, I insist that group interviews be used only to stir things up, to get us to think new thoughts we might not have otherwise considered.

A "Scientific" Way to Discover Persuasive Things to Say

When a copywriter and I have divergent ideas on how to sell a product, how can it be sorted out? For a women's product, for example, do we decide that a woman copywriter knows best because she is a woman or that I am right because I am the boss? And what about the client who believes his amazing new meal-in-a-bun will sell because it has been pre-browned for today's microwave oven?

My favourite way to sort out the appeal of various ideas is what I call the "Positioning Probe Test." I use this name to remind agency people and clients that this step should be taken *before* any final decision on positioning. Some researchers call it a "promise test," others a "concept test." Here is how our method works. All of the ideas about the product or service that the client and the agency have been able to come up with are made into simple statements. We try to keep to only one idea per statement and to eliminate "advertise-y" ways of saying things. These statements are typed on cards, one per card. The cards are shuffled and handed to the person being interviewed. In front of the interviewee on, say, a coffee table, is a board that looks like this:

We do this test on fifty to a hundred respondents. You can do more than that but won't find out much more in any market. If you were a respondent, the researcher would say something like this: "On these cards are a number of different statements. If you see one you agree with very much, place the card under the largest YES. If you disagree very much put it under the big NO. If you are fairly interested put it under the middle-sized YES, and if you are just a little interested, under the smallest YES." The explanation goes on for the remaining NO's.

When the cards are all sorted you end up with piles of cards with statements under the various YES's and NO's. Then the interviewer asks you *why* you put the statements under the big YES - and writes down your reasons for each statement. The same with the statements under the big NO. This way we find out which ideas about the product really interest you the most, which the least, and *why you accept or reject them*. This is very important reading for the copywriter. If a lot of consumers say that it is very important that an instant rice is "ready in five minutes," you may think you have a winning idea. But if you find that the reasons people give for putting that statement at the top are things like, "That's why I use it," "I expect that," etc., you have to be wary. Something like 80 per cent of women have used an instant rice, and although they realize speed is important, telling people what they already know is not always a good selling tactic. Under the big NO, you will get responses like "Stupid" and "Don't believe." But I have found help here when a lot of the answers said, "Good if true."

Research Is Often a Disaster Check

The Positioning Probe Test can protect you from dangerous mistakes. The London Life people were proud of the fact they had been in business since the 1800's. We tested this idea and it proved to be of no interest whatsoever to consumers. They *were* interested in the idea that "If you start young, you can double your money with London Life."

Clairtone was a manufacturer of stereo sets made in Canada and sold in both Canada and the States. We tested the statement "Made in Canada by Canadian craftsmen." It was the very worst idea among Canadian prospects. In the States it did much better - the Canadian attitude. In this day of ready-made foods of all kinds, when we tested ideas for spaghetti sauce, we found that women still prefer to add their own ingredients to make their own personal spaghetti sauce. A "ready-made" emphasis in the advertising would not have sent women rushing to the supermarket.

When we started to work with Fiat in Canada, the car had been presented as a very sporty, *masculine* car that could perform feats of strength, such as leaping over canals. We listened to groups of car owners discussing their reasons for choosing a make. They were far more interested in how the car was built and the resulting *control* they had as drivers. They were concerned with *safety*. If we had not listened to consumers we could easily have been seduced by the sheer *fun* of the macho approach. We would have been dramatizing a feature of little interest to intelligent car buyers.

Finding Out If a Commercial Is Persuasive

When you have discovered the idea that turns people toward your product, then you have to turn it into a commercial or an advertisement. A fertile creative person will usually think of many ways to make an ad or a commercial. The commercial may be a little playlet like a detergent message, a product demonstration, or a song-and-dance routine. The problem is to find which type will be most persuasive.

When presented with alternatives some advertisers go with their own judgement. Others will pre-test to find whether people *understand* what the commercial is trying to say. Some wait until the commercial is finished, run it on the air, and find out whether people *remember* what it said (a dubious exercise, since there appears to be no connection between recollection and selling power).

To make test commercials, we often make still photographs of people in the office acting out the story. These still photographs are copied onto movie film or tape along with voices. The result is a film that sounds and looks roughly like a commercial as you would see it on TV, except that people's mouths do not move nor do soft drinks pour or dancers dance. I have sometimes noticed that these homemade commercials seem to work more effectively on consumers than the finished commercials.

The people who specialize in making commercials on motion picture film and tape, as well as the agency creative people who are dazzled by technique, are convinced that the essence of film is *movement*, that the one way to convey an idea is through motion. I have never agreed completely with this view. I contend that the characteristic of film that separates it from other means of mass communication is that *film presents a series of images in the order in which you choose to present them.*

People *remember* still pictures. In one university research study, students were shown 2,000 slides. Hours or days later they were shown the same set of slides but with a few slides replaced by other similar slides. In 80 per cent of the cases, the students spotted the differences. There is something fixative about still pictures.

It is entirely possible to tell most stories with a series of still pictures. Motion is a convenient bonus that is often misused, overused, or used distractingly. People want to *see* what you are selling. It is annoying to the viewer when you make the image drift across the screen or yank it away before she gets a good look at it. Once, a creative person praised a baby food commercial to me. The pretty baby images floated before the eye, gracefully sliding off one corner of the screen and appearing in another. I tore a picture of a baby from a women's magazine, and moved it in front of the creative person's eyes, slowly moving it in graceful circles so she could not get a good look at it. Suddenly she realized that she did not want to see the page moving around the way they do in TV commercials. She wanted to get a good look at that baby.

We were so impressed with the effectiveness of still pictures in our test commercials that we used stills to make on-air commercials to introduce the Metrecal Slimming Plan. The sales reached their peak while we were using this simple form of advertising.

Testing the Commercial for Persuasion

A commercial is usually tested to find whether you understand it, if you remember it, or if you like it. But few are tested to find how likely you are to switch to the brand being advertised. *The one reason for the commercial's existence is rarely measured anymore.* Advertising people, especially creative people, would really rather not know whether their message will persuade people to switch brands. Sometimes test commercials are shown to groups of people and discussed as if it were a consciousness-raising session. Copywriters, art directors, account executives, and brand people watch through the one-way mirror and listen and persuade themselves that they are "on the right track."

In past years there have been many attempts at assessing persuasiveness in commercials developed by Horace Schwerin, George Gallup, and people using cameras to record pupil dilation, eye movement, and the electrical conductivity of the viewers' skin. Some may have worked. Most had some bugs. Almost all have disappeared because, I fear, they were too brutally hard on "creative" commercials. I had two of the highest brand-switching scores for Lever Brothers margarines using the Schwerin method.* One showed margarine melting on a cob of corn during the entire commercial. The other had a woman reading the vitamin content off the side of the margarine package.

"The Market Basket"

A research technique we evolved at Ogilvy & Mather in Toronto to measure brand-switching borrowed bits and pieces from various methods. We called it "the market basket."

Let us suppose you are sauntering through your shopping centre one day and a young woman holding a clipboard approaches you and asks you to pass your judgement on a television show. In the TV room, you are told that "In exchange for giving us your views, you have a chance on a draw for our market basket of products. You can choose from one to six packages from each category to a total of twenty." You notice they are offering Tide and Omo, Minute Rice and Uncle Ben's, Rowntree chocolate malt bars and Mars bars, Schweppes ginger ale and Canada Dry ginger ale, Ban Roll-On deodorant and Secret deodorant.

You make your selection - six Tide (you can always use that), two Uncle Ben's rice, two Mars bars (never *heard* of Rowntree's chocolate malt bars), three Canada Dry, one Schwéppes (just to try it), and three each of Ban and Secret. Then they show you a short, rather bland TV show with some commercials in it - some made with drawings and still photos - for Minute Rice and Rowntree's chocolate malt bars. You are asked your opinion of the show and leave with the promise you will be phoned if you win the draw.

The next day the woman from the research company calls. You think you might have won the draw but she just wants to ask some more questions. She asks if you remember the commercials, what they said.

---

* In the Schwerin test, members of an audience were asked which products they would choose from a list before being shown a TV program that included commercials. After seeing the show, and commercials, they were asked if they wished to change their choice of products.

Then she asks if you would like to change the product selection in your market basket for the draw. You think, yes, you'd like to try a couple of those Rowntree chocolate malt bars and they gave you a good idea in the Minute Rice commercial so you would switch your rice packages to Minute Rice.

That whole rigmarole is repeated with from fifty to a hundred people, chosen because mostly they were women with families, in the right age group, working or not. (They ask in advance.) What we end up with is a "vote" for the products we are interested in - ours and competitors' - *before* these home purchasing agents have seen our test commercials. And then, the next day, we get a second "vote." If there is some switching of brands, we can feel our commercial (a) was remembered for at least one day, and (b) persuaded some people to switch brands. (Note that we are not asking if they *liked* the commercials, or if they were good or bad commercials.)

The market basket method for finding whether a commercial is persuasive is one of the most useful I have ever used. Why did it disappear? Several reasons: the creative people hated it because it subjected their creative babies to the spotlight glare of *results*; our research people crumbled under the outrage of our creative people and abandoned the method; and it was an expensive technique, the cost of which, in those days, was borne by the agency. In that era, we considered research as a part of the cost of creating effective advertising. We expected to be judged on sales results. The method was allowed to die.

A similar form of measuring persuasion, I understand, is being sold today in the U.S. by Mapes & Ross of Princeton, New Jersey. There is a great need for good, objective measurement of the persuasive power of commercials today. Advertisers should insist on it - and pay for it. The cost of running ineffective commercials is enormous and wasteful. Consumers should insist that advertising be tested for effectiveness because when advertising money is wasted, the consumer pays for it.

Persuasiveness and Memorability

Studies by objective researchers have not been able to discover a relationship between a commercial's memorability and its selling powers. Some advertisers make "day-after recall" (what you remember about a commercial) their major criterion for judging a commercial. Sometimes it works, for there are very successful marketers among them.

I cannot but feel that remembering a persuasive sales argument is better than not remembering it. Perhaps these successful advertisers have buttoned down the other things that work to make a good, persuasive selling message and wrap it up by measuring its memorable qualities.

The Test Market

New commercial approaches and new products are often given one final trial in a "test market." The idea is to hive off a part of the population and broadcast your new commercial to them and see whether they rush out to buy your product more enthusiastically than people who see your old commercial.

Today, with cable TV and broad coverage by other media, it is becoming more difficult to choose an isolated city or region untouched by the rest of the world.

In the past, Peterborough, Kingston, Kitchener, and London in Ontario were sufficiently cut off from civilization that you could test new products and new commercials. Several years ago in Peterborough, New Blue Cheer was being introduced in condensed form (like All detergent) and Coke was trying out the new giant-sized bottles now sold everywhere. I thought at the time that the people in Peterborough would have a warped view of the world with miniaturized Cheer and giant-sized Coke.

Successful disaster. We distributed small plastic pouches of Softique bath oil attached to an ad in a Kingston newspaper. Two results: (1) We heard that the Kingston water works noted a peak of water usage (presumably for baths) the night the samples of Softique were delivered. (2) The weight of the stacks of newspapers caused the pouches on the bottom to burst, perfuming many copies. Whether it is for a TV commercial or a newspaper ad, a test market helps one discover many problems beyond imagination.

Now's the time to start using Softique regularly. It prevents irritating skin dryness caused by weather and indoor heating.

HOW WAS YOUR SOFTIQUE BATH?

Saturday, we gave you a sample of new Softique Bath Oil. Don't you agree it leaves you femininely soft and smooth all over?

WE HOPE you used your sample of Softique Bath Oil because soap and water dries out your skin's natural moistening oils.

And so does the weather as well as dry indoor heating.

Softique replaces those *lost* skin oils—stops you feeling dry and itchy.

A remarkable dissolving ingredient spreads Softique all through your bath water — moisturizes your skin *evenly* and completely.

What's more, Softique's moisturizing oils *protect* your skin from the drying effects of weather and heating.

Use new Softique in every bath and *prevent* irritating skin dryness.

P.S. We're sure you noticed Softique's delightfully light and lingering fragrance — and how it makes an ordinary bath *luxurious*.

Soap and water, weather and indoor heating dry out your skin oils. Your skin feels dry and itchy.

New Softique Bath oil replenishes your natural skin oils — stops irritating skin dryness.

Notice how Softique's moisturizing oils spread *all through* your bath water to moisturize skin evenly.

After a bath with Softique you feel femininely soft and smooth all over. Use Softique with a shower, too.

Softique is a new product from *Bristol-Myers*. It is available at all stores in three sizes, $1.69, $2.69 and $3.39. Now that you've tried your free sample, buy a bottle and use Softique in *every* bath.

58

To attract drivers to buy gasoline, service stations used to offer car-type gifts - safety flares, for example - appealing to men. I conceived this sales promotion idea to bring drivers back again and again to collect a set of steak knives. It is the most successful sales promotion idea I ever had. Shell sold millions of extra gallons of gasoline; dealers gave away 25 million knives. One secret of success - this was a gift appealing to women. Other successes: sets of glassware, grapefruit spoons.

We used to use test markets to evaluate the power of give-aways for Shell. We started out with the idea that our little gifts should appeal to men - things like golf balls, road flares, flashlights. It turned out that the gifts with the most strength were things that women would want - steak knives, grapefruit spoons, glassware. These were easy to test in markets like Winnipeg, Kitchener, and Kingston because we used direct mail.

One hazard of testing these days is that your competitor knows immediately what you are doing and, as often as not, will pour in extra advertising and offer tempting price-off coupons and other dastardly tricks to spoil your test and, they hope, scare you off.

Test marketing is the ultimate trial before going national. Some advertisers believe that anything less than a province-wide test, for as long as a year, is inadequate. Other advertisers will go for testing in selected communities for a couple of months. The cost of research, however, often makes it unlikely that most agencies or advertisers will do any but the bare minimum. Sadly, this lumps advertising with many other industries in Canada, where research and development spending lags behind that of Europe and Japan. Still, if I have to choose one, and only one, kind of research to help in the development of advertising, I will always opt for the Positioning Probe Test. It gives the most usable results for the lowest cost.

CHAPTER 5

An Advertising Campaign Is Born

Here is the story of an advertising campaign that illustrates how some of the departments of an advertising agency worked together to create a campaign.

A manufacturer of pantyhose hired us to advertise his product. Pantyhose were an idea whose time had come, concurrent with the miniskirt. Women were saying they didn't know which had done more to liberate women, the Pill or pantyhose. But nobody in the business knew what women were buying, or why. In a speech to the distressed Foundation Garment Industry of Canada, around that time, I said, "Sales of brassieres are off - from 9 per cent for bandeaux bras to 50.4 per cent for longline strapless. Girdles off 23.8 per cent and pantie girdles 10 per cent. I can understand garter belts and panty girdles falling off because of pantyhose. Strapless brassieres have dropped dramatically. It's my hunch that women who were daring enough to wear strapless are now daring enough to wear nothing at all."

They were times to try men's souls.

Finding the Position for Pantyhose

We set about to explore the mysteries of pantyhose. The first step in selling a product is to learn about the needs of the people who will buy it. The agency - account people, creative people, and research people - studied the newly created pantyhose market as thoroughly as possible: who is the competition? how much is bought in department stores,

60

women's wear shops, grocery stores? what kind of underwear is selling in various regions of the country?

Our research department phoned women and invited them to attend group interviews in our boardroom. These groups of young women sat around and gossiped about panties and whether people looked up your skirt on stairways. They were quite unconcerned by the TV camera that was recording their discussion on tape and piping it into a TV set in another room. There, an account executive, a woman copywriter, and I were viewing. (We always *tell* people they are being recorded. The "hidden" camera is only hidden to the extent that it won't be intrusive.)

In our pantyhose interviews we learned quickly that women liked the sense of freedom these new products gave them. We got more ideas, too. I, for example, was convinced that the hard-nosed consumer would be most impressed by the long-lasting quality of our client's pantyhose. The copywriter was sure that women chose pantyhose because of their sex appeal.

Most of the people who create advertising for women's fashion and cosmetic products are women. If you have ever felt odd about the sexiness of "Does she or doesn't she? - Only her hairdresser knows for sure," just remember it was conceived by a woman. When Braniff painted its planes pink and puce and dressed its flight attendants in seductive outfits, the dashing Mary Wells was behind it all. Many detergent commercials, probably all feminine hygiene commercials, and the bulk of food commercials are dreamed up by women.

Creative people are so convinced of the universality of their ideas and opinions, I welcome the objectivity of our Positioning Probe Test. Who was I to argue with a woman copywriter about which features of pantyhose would persuade women to choose our brand?

Finding Persuasive Ideas

For our Positioning Probe Test for pantyhose the copywriter and I started writing down ideas:

- Men are attracted to the way girls look in these pantyhose.
- These pantyhose are so good, even the top U.S. stores, like Sak's Fifth Avenue, are now carrying them.
- These pantyhose are designed by Yves St. Laurent, famous Paris couturier.
- The "nude" style in these pantyhose gives you the sexy look of wearing nothing at all.
- You never have to worry about these pantyhose slipping, because they're made with a wider elastic waistband.
- Because they're knit from a high-tension yarn, these pantyhose will never bag at your knee or ankle.

- These pantyhose are worn by many of the top fashion models in Canada.
- These pantyhose are not pre-shaped. They look kind of ugly in the package, but they give you a much better fit.

(These ideas are not in the order in which women like them, but more in the order in which we thought of them. See if you will be able to set your mind back a few years and guess how women *did* rate the statements.)

- You can count on these pantyhose to be free of flaws, because every pair is inspected at three different stages before it leaves the factory.
- These pantyhose were designed so you can always tell which is the left foot and which is the right.
- The elastic band at the top of these pantyhose won't dig into your waist.
- If you ever find a flaw in a new pair of these pantyhose, you can return them to the company and they'll send you another pair free.
- These pantyhose are made with extra stretch to ensure a smoother clinging fit on your legs.
- You get extra freedom of movement with these pantyhose, because they go only up to your hip bone.
- These pantyhose are extra long-wearing and hard to run because they're made from a special strength yarn.
- These pantyhose will never bag at your ankle.

In the early days of pantyhose, there was a different knit for the panty part and the leg part and the panty section came a couple of inches down the thigh. Our client had just developed what he called a "bikini" panty part that began higher up the thighs. This, he thought, might be a salable feature. While the copywriter and I were labouring over Positioning Probe statements, a young woman secretary came in and said, "The reason I like these pantyhose is because the panty line is really high so when you bend over, people can't see it."

I said, "Hey, let's stick that in. You never know what will work." The copywriter said I could stick it where I wanted. So I wrote down:

- You can wear these pantyhose under the miniest skirts because the pantyline is very, very short.

We tested thirty-six statements about pantyhose. I've listed seventeen. You have no doubt guessed that the idea from the young secretary led all the rest. The worst idea of all was the (fictional) idea that the pantyhose were designed by a Paris couturier. We made up this idea to discover whether a fashion leader would be impressive. We find that famous people are often not persuasive in advertising. Sexiness and attractiveness to men were not popular ideas. Long wear, good value, guarantee, and special construction did very well.

The copywriter did not care much for my methods, and she said these results proved she was right. "Let's see how they react when they can *see* what we're talking about in some ads."

Experimental Ads Gauge Women's Reactions

So we mocked up eleven advertisements based on winning and losing ideas. The art department spent a cheerful afternoon photographing a leggy model for the test ads. The copywriter refused to be bothered with the ridiculous idea about the pantyline. For test purposes I revised a headline I had used years before for Resdan, a dandruff preventive. "Banish dandruff forever" became "Banish rear view worries." Here are eight of the ad mock-ups we tested on women.

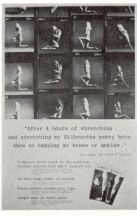

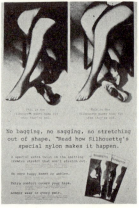

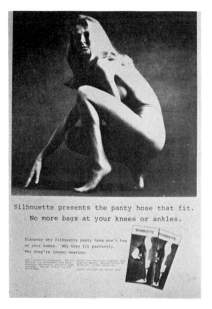

Silhouette presents the panty hose that fit.
No more bags at your knees or ankles.

Discover why Silhouette panty hose won't bag
at your knees. Why they fit perfectly.
Why they're longer wearing.

Silhouette announces
the first practical nude panty hose.

No-panty-line sheerness right up to
your waist. Sew durable enough for
you to wear every single day of the week.

At last, the show is over.

We are most happy to introduce panty hose
with a really, really short panty line.

They're made by Silhouette. The people
who believe that the centre of attention
should be nothing but you.

Banish
rear view
worries.

Silhouette has come up with
a sheer-to-the-waist
panty hose that most girls
will find wear and fit like
regular panty hose.

(If you still want the
regular kind, Silhouette
has shortened the line
on those too.)

Once again, our secretary's out-of-sight pantyline won. The copy-writer was consoled because her ad came a close second, and one of my favourite ideas, the "72-hour fit test," was the worst of all. And the tug of war, used by sales people to demonstrate the product's resilience, was another of my pet ideas that fared poorly. We used fictitious names in the research. Here is the final advertisement as it appeared in the newspapers.

The final advertisement. The name of the product was changed after testing.

This little story tells, in a simplified way, how many advertising ideas come about when an agency works in a disciplined way. The task was made easier because the manufacturer did not have layers of marketing people. You see the creative process at work and you must see that it is not very creative in the artistic sense. You see that it is nearly impossible to tell where a good idea will come from, that one's own pet ideas can turn out to be terribly wrong, and that great ideas can bounce in from nowhere. You see that the client, the copywriter, and I all had ways we thought the consumer could be persuaded to buy the product. And you see that the consumers chose their own advertising appeal, rejected the Paris couturier, rejected sex appeal, rejected questionable torture tests, and chose simple, common-sense reasons for preferring this brand of pantyhose.

Each of the ideas tested was a reasonable one. We might easily, without testing, have persuaded ourselves to gallop off in any of those directions. Sex appeal is used to sell perfumes, and at least a sexy look is used to sell Hanes pantyhose. The Italian automobile designer, Pininfarina, has been invoked to sell cars. The torture test has done well by Timex and Teflon pans over the years. Yet, at the time when pantyhose were on the rise, the pretty underview was a very appealing characteristic. According to the women who were buying them, anyhow.

CHAPTER 6

The Product Makes the Advertising

From everything I have seen, what women want most in advertising is information, facts, reasons why. They often are annoyed by or indifferent to advertising that tries to get away with being entertainment. Silly, funny, factless advertising, while popular, is not as effective as serious, plain-spoken, and even competitive advertising. (In the long run, I believe, advertising that is mostly entertainment is basically against the consumer's interest.)

In the advertising subculture, many believe the consumer is not interested in the product; or that she is too stupid, obtuse, or lazy to understand hard facts; or that the product story is too boring. These people fill the newspapers and TV screens with cartoons, puns, eye-catching moments of life, and their own favourite music in the belief that if you laugh at, are puzzled by, titillated by, or sung to with a message then you will be persuaded to buy. There is no evidence that I know of that any of these beliefs is true. The evidence, in fact, is more to the contrary.

In group interviews, in research, women have clear and strong opinions about products. They will talk your arm off about frozen desserts, floor cleaners, shampoos, shortening. Try this sometime: say to a social gathering, "I believe all detergents are the same." If you don't have a heated hour's discussion on your hands you can be sure it is a very strange gathering. I've tried it with groups of men *and* women friends with equally stimulating results. Most women are keenly interested in the products they buy and what they will do. If you find this hard to believe, you may be suffering from the Martini Illusion.

Product Attributes

In the search for the persuasive argument, I have always found the first place to look for the advertising message is within the product itself. In most cases, *the product makes the advertising*. Essentially, competition is among products, not among clever advertising messages.

Follow the Metrecal plan below and you can become one of these happy, carefree persons who never worry about their weight.

New Metrecal* slimming plan helps you lose up
to 10 lbs. in three weeks—quite pleasantly

Forget all your old ideas about dieting. Entirely new Metrecal tastes like a milkshake! And has important vitamins, minerals and proteins to help keep you looking vibrant and alive while you get those pounds off.

There are probably less than 10 lbs. between you and the swim-suit figure you'd like to have this summer.

You can get those few pounds off quite easily—and pleasantly. In fact, in three weeks you can achieve a significant weight loss. Just follow this plan. It doesn't mean a starvation diet!

To get the pounds off

Substitute Metrecal for your breakfast and lunch each day. Use Metrecal liquid, powder or wafers. (Most people prefer our new liquid *milkshake* flavours.)

Make your third meal of the day a hearty one with proper nutritional balance. Appetizing dinner menus for one week are illustrated. As you can see,

there is lots of variety in these meals.

6 new milkshake flavours

Taste what's happened to Metrecal!

Entirely new Metrecal tastes just like a milkshake. The reason? We now use concentrated protein from *fresh* milk.

There are six tempting flavours—all new Cherry, all new Banana, new Dutch Chocolate, new Chocolate, new Vanilla and new Butterscotch. They're all so delicious you'll actually look forward to a Metrecal meal!

Follow our new plan and you'll be surprised how easy it is to get those few pounds off. You'll feel happier and look more vibrant, too.

A word of caution. Alcoholic beverages

are loaded with calories. Make them taboo while you diet.

New 1200 calorie daily diet consisting of: breakfast, one can Metrecal (225 calories). Lunch, one can Metrecal (225 calories). Snack, glass skim milk and apple or orange (about 150 calories). Choose remaining meal from one of these 600 calorie menus.

SUNDAY 1 glass tomato juice, roast lamb (⅓ lb. after cooking), ½ cup mashed potatoes, ½ cup carrots, small green salad, muffin with 1 tsp. butter or margarine, 1 pear or orange, black coffee or tea.

MONDAY 1 cup beef bouillon with 4 crackers, ¼ lb. assorted cold cuts, 1 cup string beans, ½ cup turnips, roll with 1 tsp. butter or margarine, ½ cantaloupe, black coffee or tea.

TUESDAY ½ medium grapefruit, 1 cup spaghetti with sauce made from ¼ lb. minced beef, tomato paste and 1 tsp. oil, salad, lettuce, tomato, celery, green pepper) 1 cup rhubarb or raspberries (sugar-free), black coffee or tea.

WEDNESDAY Shrimp cocktail (¼ lb. cooked shrimp), salad made with lettuce, slice tomato, tangerine or orange, 1 tsp. cream cheese, ½ cup potato salad, 1 muffin, 1 cup strawberries (sugar-free), black coffee or tea.

THURSDAY 1 glass tomato juice, ⅓ lb. pork chops (broiled), ⅓ cup apple sauce, 1 small boiled potato, ½ cup onions, 1 cup cabbage, roll with 1 tsp. butter or margarine, black coffee or tea.

FRIDAY 1 glass orange juice, ⅓ lb. fish fillet, ½ cup lima beans, 1 cup broccoli, small green salad, 1 muffin, 1 cup strawberries (sugar-free) with 1 tbsp. cream, black coffee or tea.

SATURDAY 1 cup clear broth with 4 crackers, roast or broiled chicken (¼ lb. after cooking), a small baked potato, 1 cup asparagus, ½ cup green peas, 1 slice bread with 1 tsp. butter or margarine, ½ medium grapefruit, black coffee or tea.   *T.M. Reg'd*

FREE: For a pamphlet describing other 600 calorie menus write to Miss B. Henderson, Edward Dalton Company, Box 533, Station F, Toronto, Ont.

"Lose up to 10 lbs. in three weeks" was the optimum consumers found realistic. A more severe diet could have promised more weight loss, an easier diet would take longer. We found the most acceptable combination through research with women. Metrecal sales soared to new heights.

At last, twentieth century science has developed a dresser drawer that won't stick.

You'll find this and twelve other horse-sense ideas in every Imperial Loyalist dresser.

The product makes the advertising. In research, women said that the most important idea about dressers was that the drawers didn't stick. The overall best idea for Imperial furniture was that the finish was so tough even nail polish wouldn't hurt it and you could wash it with soap and water. Facts sell.

In most of the instances I know, because I made the advertising myself or understood how it was developed, the product determined the message. Here are a few examples:

- Good Luck tastes so good you have to be *told* it's margarine.*
- Lipton soups taste homemade because you cook them youself.*
- Hellman's Real Mayonnaise tastes good because it's made with whole eggs.*
- Noxzema skin cream is medicated.
- Coffee Crisp makes a nice light snack.*
- Each Aero chocolate bar has the nourishment of almost three ounces of milk.*
- You can lose up to ten pounds in three weeks with the Metrecal Slimming Plan.*
- Ban won't wear off as the day wears on.**
- Campbell's tomato soup has the flavour of fresh tomatoes.*
- If you start young with London Life Insurance, you can double your money.*
- You can make interesting variations with Minute Rice by using consommé, tomato juice, or apple juice in place of water.*

---

* Product messages of my own development.

** Product messages developed under my creative direction.

- Softique bath oil makes you soft and smooth all over, naturally.**
- Shell gasoline has nine ingredients for top performance.
- To get those things that really count, just say "Charge it" on your Eaton's account.**
- Some gins have rather strong flavouring. Others are utterly tasteless. Gilbey's London Dry has the perfect balance for mixed drinks.*
- Carefree tampons protect up to three times longer.**
- Johnson & Johnson J-Cloths have 1001 uses.**

Each of these advertising campaigns grew out of the product. Each was factual, common-sense, informative. Every one of them worked.

When Advertising Makes the Product

There are exceptions to my belief that the product makes the advertising. Most of the exceptions have little to do with women in their role as purchasing agents for the family. They are more aimed at men and may strengthen my hypothesis that women are more rational consumers than men are.

Cigarettes, soft drinks, beers, and spirits are the most evident exceptions. I have named this kind of product a *badge product.**** You "wear" a badge product to show what kind of person you are. In these unusual cases, the advertising makes the product. When a person guzzles a Coke, or cracks a can of Labatt's Blue or Miller's, or asks for Smirnoff or Dubonnet, that person is telling friends and those strangers within earshot just what kind of person he (or she) thinks he (or she) is.

When you pull out a pack of duMaurier or Export A, you reveal your personality, your self-image. When I helped introduce Rothman's cigarettes into Canada we worked with a social psychologist the manufacturer hired to explore the cigarette smoker's motivations. He drew us a chart of the kinds of people who smoked the various brands. At the time, the cancer connection was fresh news. Filter-tips were smoked by a minority. Filter smokers were seen as effete, upper-class, scaredy-cat people. They used namby-pamby brands such as Viceroy and duMaurier. "Hard rocks" stuck to harsh cigarettes like Export.

Strangely, for all the psychological mystique hinted at by the

---

* Product messages of my own development.

** Product messages developed under my creative direction.

*** I have heard other people use the expression "badge product" to me, even explain it to me. It is a dubious distinction to have put another buzz-word expression into the marketing lexicon.

research, and expensive research it was, none of the findings influenced the Rothman chief honcho's thinking a jot. The advertising, for twenty years, has consisted of a hand holding a Rothman's package (the sleeve looking vaguely military) or a package nestled among golden tobacco leaves, with the statement that "Rothman's King Size really satisfies." Rothman's, by the way, *did* have a product story. It was the first king-sized cigarette to be sold in Canada at regular prices.

I learned from the cigarette people that, for a badge product, the *package design* was perhaps the most important part of the product. Of the advertising, too. Rothman, without indulging in advertising showing beautiful people, young "with-its," or rugged cowboys, became and has remained a dominant cigarette brand in Canada as well as in the U.K., Australia, and the Middle East.

Soft drinks are very much badge products. Daring is the teen who would order a Royal Crown Cola when the rest of the pack barks, "Coke." And yet . . . Pepsi cracked the Coca-Cola grip on the throats of the nation with "the Pepsi Challenge" - a product story. (This is an advertising approach I wish I had invented myself.) Pepsi-Cola, in fact, was introduced to the world many years ago with a product value story (to the tune of "D'ye ken John Peel," an old English folksong).

Pepsi-Cola hits the spot
Twelve whole ounces, that's a lot.
Twice as much for a nickel too,
Pepsi-Cola is the drink for you.

I think the jingle tinkled off to a chorus of "nickel, nickel, nickel."
It is hardly necessary to dilate on beer as a badge product.

Cars and Women's Fashions

Two other product categories do not precisely fit into my feeling that the product makes the advertising: (1) automotive, and (2) women's fashions and cosmetics. Among all of the influences on the choice of a car in North America, advertising plays a small part. It is the car itself, as it zips past you on the highway, as it sits in your lawyer's parking space, as your best friend drives up in it, as your worst enemy gets out of hers at the hairdresser's - the car itself does most of the selling. The product *is* the advertising.

The automobile is a mobile, 3-D advertisement, complete with testimonials and "positioning" background. As I drive to and from my office, I see 50,000 of these perambulating advertisements a day. There is more effective advertising circulation of the Mustang itself in the streets than there is in all the TV commercials and newspaper and magazine advertisements for the car.

Although you should never drive at that speed, the Lancia Beta Coupe will do a dignified 160 km/h (over 100 m.p.h.). Remarkable gas mileage. With 5-speed stick shift around $9,400... some dealers may sell for even less.

Sex and the Lancia Beta Coupe.

Twenty percent of the Lancia production line workers are women.

Despite female chauvinists, the Lancia people find there are certain things women can do better than men. They are convinced that women have sharper eyes, steadier hands and infinitely more patience than men, that they are painstaking with upholstery, adept at finicky electrical installation, perfectionists with trim.

In fact, a large proportion of the people on the line are more artisans than mere bolt tighteners. They meticulously hand-buff, sand, file and smooth the metal to a finish inconceivable with mere metal stamping machines.

Needless to say, the rate of production is modest — about 300 cars a day.

It is Lancia's history of perfection that makes it a name Europeans class easily with Mercedes and Jaguar. A test drive is worth 1000 words.

"Sex and the Lancia Beta Coupe." I was tempting fate with that headline. The denouement in the text was that women did certain skilled jobs on the production line. If I were asked to choose my best-looking campaign of the past five years, the Lancia campaign would be it.

Advertising is a very small part of the cost of a car. The manufacturers spend more on door locks than they do on advertising. The car business is so big that the amount of their advertising dominates TV and publications. Because advertising is such a small portion of the influences that cause you to choose one car over another, automotive advertising has never become very sophisticated or responsive to consumer reaction. Advertising is used to introduce new models, remind you that the car is there, and keep dealers happy. It is likely, even, that what car dealers like - what *they* believe is good advertising - has more influence on the shape of car advertising than does the need of the buyers. That probably explains the little sexpots in the TV commercials even though about 40 per cent of cars are now being bought by women.

Exception to the exception: Mercedes-Benz carved a place for itself with factual, low-key product advertising. With a small advertising budget and a great product it has steadily gained a reputation in Canada and the United States.

At Ogilvy & Mather I started writing Mercedes-Benz advertising in Canada when it was a rusty little foreign car whose diesel engine went "poketa, poketa." By the time I moved on, Mercedes was being compared with Rolls Royce (though not necessarily as a result of my efforts), and today Cadillac people are switching *up* to Mercedes. As people grow more value-conscious (and perhaps because an increasing number of women are making the buying decision on cars) other car advertisers are emulating Mercedes by telling a thorough product story. Even Ford is reciting product attributes at length.

Advertising for cosmetics does not usually appeal to reason. I *have* sold beauty products with a rational argument. We told women how to care for their skins using Noxzema skin cream. Noxzema was the number-one product in the cleansing-cream business. We told women with great success how Softique bath oil would keep skin from drying. But otherwise I have done little work in that magical world of lipsticks, perfumes, lotions, and creams.

A Case History: A Product that Made Persuasive Advertising

I have made advertising for hundreds of different products, from the world's first transparent corn plaster through detergents, ice creams, canned ravioli, and frozen puff pastries to liqueurs. If I had to choose one product story that illustrates the applications of my thesis that the product makes the advertising, I would hold up my experience with Campbell's soups. For generations Campbell had towered above everyone else in food marketing. There were cans of Campbell's soup

72

in something like 70 per cent of Canadian kitchens. Campbell's advertising sold *soup as a good thing*, probably in the belief that if people bought more soup, about 70 per cent of it would be Campbell's.

When I started to look at the people who bought soup, things were changing. At that time, the people who bought the most soup were mothers of children aged five to twelve, which made the mother's ages from thirty to forty-five. For a generation, the classic kids' lunch at home had been soup and a sandwich - easy to prepare, wholesome and nutritious. When I entered the Campbell Soup scene along with Ogilvy & Mather, mothers were being presented with a smorgasbord of new alternative foods to titillate the jaded palates of their fickle offspring: spaghetti, ravioli, instant dry soup mixes, toaster snacks, and dozens of other temptations. The air was full of advertising for products that sought to replace soup in the nation's stomachs.

We talked to mothers.

We wrote out statements about soup and had mothers tell us which were most persuasive. On the negative side, we found that women did *not* believe there was as much nutrition in canned soup as there is in homemade soup. They believed that there were less vitamins and nutrients; that canned soup was deficient in meat; that it was *watery*. (The last perception is doubtless caused by the fact you add a can of *water* to these condensed soups.)

Where can you get more nourishment for the money?

The Campbell's can is full of vegetables— <u>sixteen</u> different vegetables. A bowlful costs less than 6¢.

Sixteen vegetables in a real beefy broth made from real soup bones: Campbell's incomparable Vegetable Soup. Along with a peanut butter sandwich, a glass of milk and an apple, it makes about as nourishing a lunch as any mother could ask for.

Campbell's Vegetable Soup costs less than 6¢ a bowl, based on 2 servings from the regular size.

Two of the most successful ads I have ever written. Campbell had raised prices slightly and sales slumped. Sales turned upward immediately after this campaign appeared. Who says women are not interested in factual advertising? Don't you love those prices.

The product itself contradicted most of these beliefs. In the production of many Campbell's soups, vegetable soups for instance, the vegetables are put in the can raw or partly cooked. The can is sealed tight, and then, under high pressure, the contents are cooked. Vitamins and minerals are retained, as in a pressure cooker. If you cook in an open pot on your own stove some of the volatile vitamins can boil off into the air. I was able to say in advertising that "Campbell's soup contains more nutrition than if you cooked the soup on your own stove."

In our research, women reacted positively to statements that assured them that these soups would nourish their children. I have reasoned that women were pleased to discover that this time-saver food product was also *good* for their beloved children. Perhaps there is some guilt about food that is easy to prepare. I expect that, before long, McDonald's hamburgers will have to start to tell parents that *their* products have good food value.

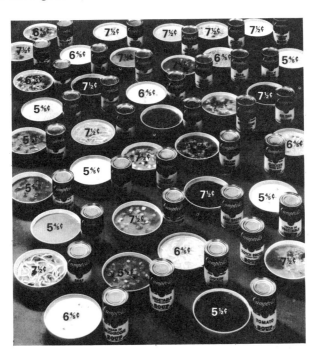

Average cost: about 6½¢ a bowl

**Campbell's Soup still remains
one of the best food buys of all time.**

Campbell makes 35 different kinds of soup. The average cost of all 35 different kinds, is about 6½¢ a bowl. That's based on three servings from the regular size and six servings from the large size. About 6½¢ a bowl—astonishingly good value.

We also got women's reactions to product facts about each *variety* of Campbell Soup. They were impressed with the number of vegetables in Campbell's vegetable soup, the real chicken meat and the noodles in chicken noodle soup, the fresh tomato taste of the tomato soup, and the cream and mushroom pieces in the mushroom soup. One surprising (in retrospect, obvious) discovery was that the more kinds of Campbell's soups a woman could name, the more soup she used.

In creating television commercials, I decided that the product would make the advertising. Rather than try to talk to women about the entire line of soups, it seemed to me we could make our point with one variety at a time. For the first year that we advertised Campbell's soups, we promoted only four varieties, just one variety at a time, each for a period of about three months.

The first soup we featured was chicken noodle. I had become convinced that people had stopped looking at the soup - that they used it automatically, out of habit. I decided to force them to *see* the product. Each Campbell TV commercial began with the can being opened. You looked into the can and the announcer said, "It is full of noodles, big, fat, slurpy noodles, the kind kids really like." The can was full to the brim with noodles and they were poured into the pot. A spoon dug into a bowl of soup and brought up some chicken meat. The soup looked so good that the Canadian Broadcasting Corporation thought we had faked the picture. The product made the advertising. Inside of four months, the sales of Campbell's chicken noodle soup had increased by 25 per cent.

To assure that the product would be the hero of the advertising, we used no actors eating soup, no humour, no fancy dishes or eye-catching cutlery or placemats. I was constantly at war with producers who kept trying to pretty up the table setting. I wanted the eye to be riveted to the spoon as it dove into the soup and brought up its load of noodles and broth - just the way your own eyes, or your children's, are fixed on the spoon to see what it discovers.

People Love to Look at Food

In magazine advertising a picture of a food - a cake, a TV dinner, a bowl of soup - by itself involves the reader more than the same product with people in the picture eating the product. I have a hunch it is much the same in TV advertising. In TV, I can hold up a piece of pie or a salad to you in your living room and it is for *you* to bite into. If *someone else* is in the picture devouring the food, it is being taken from you.

I have had a running guerrilla fight with television cameramen, directors, and producers about food advertising. They seem to feel they must use guile and frippery to make the viewer look at food. I believe that the food itself, appetizingly lighted, steaming or pouring or bubbling or melting, is absolutely the most attractive thing, the most persuasive thing, the most hungrifying thing to set before the eyes of the beholder. "If it is good enough to eat, it will *look* good enough to eat." A good food commercial should make the viewer want to take a bite out of the television screen.

Campbell's Vegetable Soup and Zippy Burgers

For an unusually nourishing lunch:
1. **Campbell's Vegetable Soup** — made with sixteen different vegetables. Processed a special Campbell way — to save flavour and valuable nutrients, as much as if you cooked them on your own stove.
2. **Zippy Burgers** — more flavour than ordinary hamburgers. More nourishment, too. And children love Zippies.

1 pound ground beef
1 tablespoon shortening
¼ cup chopped onion
¼ cup chopped celery
1 teaspoon salt
dash pepper
1 can (10 oz.) Campbell's Tomato Soup
6 hamburger buns, split and toasted.

In frying pan, brown meat in shortening. Reduce heat; add onion, celery, and seasonings. Cook until vegetables are tender. Add soup; simmer about 15 minutes stirring now and then. Serve on buns. 6 servings.

WATCH TUESDAY FOR ANOTHER LUNCH IDEA

Campbell's Vegetable Soup and "Funwiches"

Campbell's Vegetable Soup is most children's favourite. They like the bite-sized vegetables, the amusing alphabets. *Mothers* like the fact that this is a *nourishing* soup — made with 16 different vegetables and hearty stock simmered from real beef bones. "Funwiches" are sandwiches that appeal especially to youngsters. We list five. They're all surprisingly wholesome.
1. **Peanut butter and banana:** the banana can be sliced or wrapped whole, hot-dog style.

2. **Cheese and grape jelly:** make the layer of cheese thick, with just enough jelly for flavour.
3. **Bologna and pickle:** slice standard sweet pickles thinly, or use pre-sliced "bread-and-butter" pickles.
4. **Salmon salad:** mix together salmon, finely-chopped celery and onion, plus a dab of mayonnaise.
5. **Chopped egg and relish:** a dash of relish in standard, chopped egg ingredients adds colour, flavour.

WATCH TOMORROW FOR ANOTHER LUNCH IDEA

Campbell's Vegetable Soup and Cheese Breezes

You'd be doing your family a favour if you served Campbell's Vegetable Soup every day. Campbell's Vegetable Soup actually contains 16 different vegetables — processed a special Campbell way to save flavour and valuable nutrients. To complete today's menu, serve nippy, open-face "Cheese Breezes".

½ pound process cheese, grated
1 egg, slightly beaten
½ teaspoon dry mustard
6 slices bread

Blend cheese, egg, and seasoning. Spread on bread. Broil 4" from heat for 2 to 4 minutes or until cheese bubbles. 6 servings.

WATCH TOMORROW FOR ANOTHER LUNCH IDEA

Un savoureux pain de viande avec une soupe Campbell

Madame, régalez votre famille avec un savoureux pain de viande, facile à réaliser grâce à la soupe Campbell.

Pain de viande à la sauce tomate

1 boîte (10 onces) de soupe aux tomates Campbell
¼ tasse d'eau
1 tasse de croûtons
¼ tasse oignon émincé
2 c. à soupe de persil haché
1 oeuf légèrement battu

1 c. à thé de sel
⅛ c. à thé de poivre
1½ lb de boeuf haché
Mélanger soupe et eau. Combiner ½ tasse de cette soupe avec croûtons, oignon, persil, oeuf, sel et poivre. *Bien* incorporer à la viande. Former un pain; mettre dans un plat à gratin peu profond (12 x 8 x 2). Cuire à four modéré (350°) pendant 1 heure et 15 minutes. Mélanger le reste de soupe avec 2 c. à soupe de jus de cuisson. Réchauffer; remuer de temps à autre. Verser sur le pain au moment de servir. 4 à 6 portions.

MARDI, CAMPBELL VOUS PROPOSERA UN AUTRE MENU-TYPE

Recipes and menus. Most people had plenty of Campbell's soup in their pantries. We deduced that it was our job to get them to use it up so they would go out and buy some more. We ran a new recipe or soup-and-sandwich idea every weekday. Barbara Parker wrote most of these brisk, eye-catching ads.

Recipes in Advertising

Two of the four Campbell soups we chose to feature in the first year were cream of mushroom and tomato, soups that are often used in cooking. When 70 per cent of women already have your product in the kitchen, you can't expect them to buy any more until they use up what they already have. Recipes had been used for years to encourage women to use Campbell's soups. But the recipes were sometimes rather complicated, like casseroles or chicken cacciatore - really fun to read and prepare mentally, but not something you would use very often. Also, not very easy to explain on TV. It occurred to me that if one selected just one recipe for cream of mushroom soup and repeated it on TV often enough, eventually it would become second nature.

We chose the recipe in which you simply brown pork chops in a pan, add chopped onion, Campbell's cream of mushroom soup, some water, and simmer. The result is extraordinarily delicious. It was my fond hope that whenever pork chops were being cooked, it would be almost a conditioned reflex for you to add the Campbell's mushroom soup.

The Ultimate "Product-makes-the-advertising" Example

We puzzled over what to do with the fact that women who knew more names of soups bought more soups. We were not sure which came first, the chicken or the egg, but on the assumption we could not affect the chicken, we decided to take a crack at the egg. David Ogilvy suggested we *recite* all the thirty-one names of Campbell's varieties. I wrote a patter song to the cancan music from *Orpheus in the Underworld* by Offenbach. It worked. People wrote in for the lyrics. A cab driver once sang the whole song to me. It is probably the best-remembered television commercial I have done. Ten years after it was on the air there were still people who believed it had been on the air only a year or two earlier.

Imagine the lyrics accompanied by pictures of labels, cans, steaming bowls of soup. (It was a mad scramble to set out thirty-one bowls of steaming hot soup and film them before they cooled down.)

> If ever you have wondered what
> To serve for lunch that's piping hot,
> Campbell's makes an awful lot
> Thirty soups and more they've got
> There's Vegetable, Chicken Rice,
> Tomato Rice and Onion nice
> Chicken Noodle, big Beef Noodle
> Turkey Veg and Turkey Noodle,

Chicken Gumbo, hearty Beef
Chicken Veg and Veg with Beef
Cream of Chicken, Celery Cream
Cream of Mushroom, sauce supreme.
Asparagus and Green Pea too,
Clam Chowder, Cheddar Cheese - it's new
Minestrone, French Pea Soup
and zesty Consommé.
Beef Broth, Oxtail,
Bean with Bacon, Scotch Broth,
Tomato Soup, Potato Soup,
And Vegetable with Beans.
Vegetarian Vegetable, name them all
If you are able.
There are more than thirty
Different kinds of Campbell's soup!
More than thirty kinds ...
Delicious, different kinds
There is always something new
To try in Campbell's soup.

Can you imagine a simpler case of the product making the advertising?

In the marketing world, Campbell was regarded as a little backward, a trifle slow, with a quaint devotion to product quality. Young MBAs would ask, "Why use all those vegetables in the vegetable soup when most people would never know the difference?"

The Consumer Senses Product Value

It has been my good luck to work with a great many people who make good products. Campbell has been almost obsessive about product quality. Over the years competitors keep trying to unseat them. Grocery chains go to Campbell's competitors and get them to produce cheap and lower quality soups with the store's name on them. Some budget-watchers will be driven to cheaper soups at times. Some do not have the taste to tell one soup from another. But *en masse*, the consumer eventually knows where she gets the best value. Campbell, conscientiously turning out a high-quality product, still holds at bay the cheap imitations, the store brands, the no-name brands.

A few years ago, Campbell decided to adjust the quantities of vegetables in their vegetable soup in Canada to reduce the amount of turnip and carrots and increase some of the cheerier vegetables. The resulting soup *was* a shade different in flavour. So, borrowing from my detergent experience where we dramatized small product improvements, I proposed to Campbell that we introduce it as "New, improved

Vegetable Soup." When I presented the suggestion, in Camden, to Bev Murphy, then president of the Campbell Soup Company, he said, "People won't think there's that much of a difference."

"But," I said, "the soap companies say 'new, improved' all the time."

"That's the kind of thing that makes people distrust advertising," said Bev Murphy.

During one onslaught against Campbell's, the stores' brand soups were imitating Campbell's red-and-white cans. We decided to prepare advertising that would alert consumers to the difference in quality. We gathered groups of women and showed them a variety of advertising messages. One ad said in its headline, "Beware of imitations." The women were appalled. "Surely Campbell's would not stoop to *that*." Perhaps Bev Murphy had something.

I have used Campbell's soups to demonstrate how the product makes the advertising. It is popular in advertising circles today to profess that all products are alike and that the differences are created by advertising. And yet, most great marketing successes depend on products that are demonstrably superior. Procter & Gamble spends millions of dollars in research to make products like Tide and Crest and Cheer better than anything else you can buy. Kodak dominates with the best film and Polaroid competes with the easiest cameras. Kraft provides excellent cheeses and General Foods offers you several great coffees. Rowntree rose in the confectionery market on product innovations like Aero with bubbles, candy-coated Smarties (imitated in the States as M&M's), Coffee Crisp, and Kit Kat biscuit bars. In the end, the competition is not among advertising but among products.

CHAPTER 7

The Seven Basic Plots for Television Commercials

If you are anything like most of the women I hear from, you very likely see advertising as a clever plot bordering on black magic, to manipulate you, consciously or no, into buying a lot of unnecessary products. Perhaps some of your suspicions are true. But, on the whole, most advertising is fairly innocent in its intent and not very sophisticated in its execution. Television advertising is the form that most people complain about when they attack advertising.

In the days before television, advertising was a glamorous business. One was proud to be in that exciting world of famous products, newspapers, magazines, and radio stars. I was delighted to be able to say I wrote advertising for Goodyear tires, Borden's ice cream, Cheer detergent, Arrow shirts. Why has our once charismatic, prestigious business become so degraded in public opinion?

I believe the fall of advertising's reputation was precipitated by television. When advertising appeared only in newspapers and magazines, on billboards and streetcars, you could pay attention *should you choose to*. You could ignore advertising if you wished. When radio came along there was a certain amount of shouting for attention. But in those days broadcaster greed was not so highly developed. There might be one commercial at a break in the show. Never two, three, or four. Although we thought radio commercials strident and annoying, they were not so fiercely intrusive upon our consciousness as are TV commercials. We seemed to be able, still, to choose whether or not to listen. We sat *beside* the radio. The volume control was within arm's reach. We did not have to hoist the body from the chair and walk across the room in order to turn down the volume to allow conversation. You could control whether or not you listened to the message. In fact, you rather *liked* some commercials - "Rinso White," the Lucky Strike chant, "Ipana for the smile of beauty, Sal Hepatica for the smile of health."

Then came television. Suddenly you had no choice about commercials. You were watching the *Show of Shows* or *Ed Sullivan* and right in the midst of your entertainment a commercial was thrust upon you. You could get up and go to the bathroom. Many did. In the early days of television, city water-flow charts showed high tides that coincided with commercial breaks. Or you could turn and talk to your husband or guests (TV was a social pastime in its early days). Some people employed devices that turned the sound off during commercials. But most of us, too lazy to move, too tired to talk, simply sat like lumps and suffered the commercials. And hated their intrusion.

Advertisers discovered you could put two commercials into a break in the show, and then four. In the television era, the viewer held captive by inertia, in the midst of pleasant entertainment, has been bombarded with commercials that cannot be ignored. Irritation. Torture. Hatred.

Television commercials, combining motion and sound, compel attention. They are inescapable. You could ignore radio, billboards, and print advertising. But TV messages, with their penetrating presence, are put before your protesting eyes again, again, and again. You become so familiar with some commercials you learn to hate the way an actress says, "But after all, I'm worth it," the maddening automaton acting of the ladies comparing the whiteness of diapers. You become convinced that the woman's surprise at the unveiling of Brand X detergent, which at first seemed so spontaneous, is carefully rehearsed; eventually you are able to duplicate the surprised tones yourself.

(Today, more and more homes have cable and the converter. When the commercials appear, many viewers flip to another channel - usually to be met by another commercial. One can flit up and down the dial without leaving the armchair. Some people cut from show to show, watching two or three at once.)

If you view certain kinds of shows regularly, the media selection computers will make sure that you see certain commercials ten times or a hundred times more often than the person who wrote it or produced it or paid for it. It is entirely possible you will spend more time *looking* at the commercial than it took to create it. I am convinced that it is because of this enforced intimacy of television viewing that a good deal of the hatred and mythology of advertising has grown up.

Commercial Techniques

There is really very little mystery about television advertising. After you have read this chapter and the next one, you should be able not only to understand the workings of TV commercials but also to create your own if you care to. And I have no doubt many of them would be better than commercials that are on the air now. I believe that I could spend two hours telling a class of twelve-year-olds the principles of good TV commercial construction and many of them could create commercials as effective as those churned out by $60,000-a-year copywriters.

It is said that in all storytelling there are but seven plots. So it is not astonishing that in modern storytelling there are seven different forms of commercials. All commercials follow these basic forms, or are combinations of two or more.

1. *Demonstrating the product.* For me, the arrival of television was a great liberation. For years I had been trying to show people, in newspapers and magazines, how things worked. Now I had a store window in every livingroom.

When I was a boy, medicine men still worked the backwoods. I remember one who was selling penetrating linament. He applied his linament to one side of a piece of thick shoe sole leather and in moments we saw it soak through and show wet on the other side. I haven't learned much about television advertising since.

A demonstration is powerful because it can show you "texture" - the thickness of ketchup, the body in hair, the bubbles in tonic water, the feel of a Mercedes swerving at eighty miles an hour to avoid a truck, the smoothness of an instant pudding, the fluffiness of Minute Rice.

Television can do some things no other medium can do. In this commercial for Mercedes-Benz, the viewer "feels" the narrow escape made possible by the superb handling of the automobile. TV can also demonstrate the feel of lively hair, the sparkle of wine, the thickness of cream, the texture of mushroom soup as no other medium can.

When you demonstrate the product, you help the consumer *rehearse* using it. We all resist the unfamiliar. A product demonstration makes us familiar with the actions and sights to expect from a frozen pizza, a fabric softener, a video game, or a coating for baking chicken. In commercials shown in theatres and on TV in the U.K., Rowntree had long indulged in psychological situations that were built around the moments of enjoying candy - as if it were necessary to tell people what they already knew very well. This is usually called "lifestyle" advertising.

My commercial for Coffee Crisp chocolate bar was a forthright demonstration of the product. It showed a knife slicing through the bar, revealing the biscuit and bubbly, coffee-flavoured filling in full-screen magnification. The genteel Rowntree folk were horrified at this crass Canadian directness. They grudgingly allowed it to be used. Coffee Crisp swiftly became the number-one candy bar in Canada. When we were putting the commercial together, we showed the first footage to Dolores Clayman, who wrote the music for many of my commercials. When the close-up of the Coffee Crisp cross-section was revealed on the screen, she exclaimed, "I want one right now." I was pretty sure I had a successful commercial.

Kraft food demonstrations for years were consistently among the best on television. The advertising *wunderkinder* loathed Kraft commercials because they are so *uncreative*. All the commercials did was show you how to prepare easy dishes using Kraft products. The picture was always vividly sharp, the food glistening, crumbling, pouring, spreading sensuously. The Kraft people were so uncreative that all they did was make you run to the fridge for a slice of Cracker Barrel or mentally note you must buy some Philadelphia brand to make that evilly delicious fruit pie. Copywriters are repelled by such simplicity, without clever phrases, comical people, or ingenious photography.

These commercials simply asked you to look at food, something most of us do with relish two or three times a day. I have noticed that whenever Kraft makes "advertise-y" commercials for cheese slices or Miracle Whip or margarine, they are just as annoying in their silliness as anyone else's.

Kraft sales are gigantic. They can be fairly certain that, if they stimulate you to make cheeseburgers using processed cheese, they stand a good chance that the processed cheese in your refrigerator is Kraft. Very likely, you people who are educated enough to read and think prefer Brie or Stilton. But remember the Martini Illusion. People who prefer Kraft cheese slices are the norm. You are the exception.

Problem solution is a subdivision of product demonstration. You present the viewer with a problem and then demonstrate how your product solves it - split ends mended by a shampoo; perspiration stopped by a deodorant. Recent research by Mapes & Ross shows that this remains one of the most powerful ways to persuade you to switch brands.

Before and after is another form of problem solution - the sad breasts made lovely by Playtex brassieres; spiritless eyes made scintillating by Maybelline; a bored family enlivened by chicken done in "Shake 'N' Bake."

2. *Comparative demonstration.* When your product has an advantage over its competitors it is only sensible to demonstrate that superiority as unequivocally as possible. That is one thing free competition is about. It is in the interest of the public to demonstrate product differences. Consumers like a comparative demonstration, as long as it appears fair. People are sometimes upset by commercials that are too aggressive. Research shows that comparisons tend to be remembered better than the average commercial.

Probably the greatest comparative demonstration on television happened largely by a happy accident. When Ogilvy & Mather won the Shell account the previous agency was using a bug-eyed cartoon car with the slogan, "Cars Love Shell." David Ogilvy tested various appeals for gasoline and found "top performance" was best. He found that gasoline had *ingredients*, much to everyone's surprise. His advertising campaign, launched with full pages of supporting text, proclaimed that Shell gasoline has nine ingredients for top performance. (Esso sent its dealers an outraged bulletin, too late, telling them that Esso had *fourteen* ingredients.) The newspaper campaign had tremendous impact. For the first time since anti-knock ingredients, people were *reading* about gasoline.

When the advertising moved to television, the Ogilvy creative people demonstrated the ingredients, one at a time. Commercials showed how one of Shell's ingredients, TCP, stopped cars from knocking, how another ingredient kept spark plugs from becoming dirty. To demonstrate how an ingredient worked, they had gasoline formulated leaving out the ingredient. We made one of the commercials in Canada, in desperately cold Gimli, Manitoba. There, we demonstrated that *without* the easy-vapourizing ingredient, butane, engines were difficult to start in cold weather, whereas *with* butane comparable cars started easily.

One ingredient that contributed to mileage was called platformate. To demonstrate the mileage ingredient, a car was put on an unused stretch of railroad track and, in a rigidly scientific manner, without a driver to fiddle with the gas pedal or brakes, it was set off to run as far as the gasoline without platformate would take it. When the car stopped, two official-looking guards in uniform set up a large paper barrier to mark the distance the car had travelled. The car was pulled back to the starting point and filled again with an equal amount of gasoline, this time with platformate. The car was set off again. It broke through the paper and went on for miles.

The commercial was just one of a series. But in tests for persuasion and recall it was dramatically superior. It was so good that another commercial was made on the famous salt flats of Utah (used in fashion photos, car commercials and for world-record speed trials). This time white cars using gas with platformate beat black cars using gasoline without platformate. The mileage ingredient proved so compelling that we forsook all others. Almost of its own volition, Super Shell became known as the mileage gasoline. We made many commercials across Canada demonstrating mileage. The car broke through the barrier in the Atlantic Provinces, in Ottawa, in Vancouver.

In the first year I worked with Shell Canada at Ogilvy & Mather we ran ads created by the agency in New York. They were full pages of type explaining how gasoline is formulated using nine ingredients. Today, some twenty years later, many consumers who are old enough remember those advertisements vividly. The ad at right is one I wrote for Canadian use. The moulting deer was photographed in Algonquin Park.

FREE:

Shell Touring Service offers complete vacation kit—marked routes, brochures, expense records

Always, we explained that we were demonstrating Shell *with* platformate and Shell *without* platformate. Somewhere the consumer took over and assumed that we were demonstrating Shell against competitive gasolines, and that we were claiming to get better mileage than other gasolines. As this misunderstanding grew stronger, we strengthened the statement to say, "All gasolines contain a mileage ingredient. This is *not* a demonstration of competitive gasolines but a demonstration of Shell with platformate and without platformate." What could be clearer? But the visual story dominated. People assumed that Shell alone contained platformate. By accident we had a deceptive commercial on our hands. We had to abandon a comparative demonstration that became *too* effective. Not long after, the energy crisis burst upon us and gasoline advertising became redundant.

Another accident became a great memory device for me. A blindfold taste test comparing margarine and butter had been used successfully by Lever Brothers for selling margarine around the world. I was asked to try it for Good Luck margarine in Canada. The testees nibbled a cracker spread with margarine and another spread with butter. Most of them could not tell them apart. Often they identified the margarine as butter.

The women would often say, "Well, this one is butter," or "This tastes like butter." Some archaic Ontario law said we would all go to jail if anyone said the word "butter" on TV in a margarine commercial. As a temporary measure, the film editor covered up the word "butter" on the sound track with a couple of the "beeps" you sometimes hear used to signal the beginning of the sound on a film. We intended to replace the beeps with a honk or some other device usually used to obliterate obscenities from interviews. The "beep beep" sound caught our fancy so we left it in. After the commercials had been on the air some time, people were saying, "Please pass the beep beep." A dairy's junior hockey team named itself the "Butter Beeps." What is more, Good Luck margarine sales leaped ahead.

At Young & Rubicam, we used a similar comparative taste test in which we challenged women to compare Lipton tea with their favourite brand. On the average, Lipton was preferred by nine out of ten women. This test, and probably most other taste tests, depends on the fact that your first cup of tea tastes most delicious. After that, your taste buds become a little insensitive and the second cup of tea seems relatively tasteless. If you take care to have the brand you are advertising tasted first, you will be pretty sure of winning the day.

In beer taste-testing, most people are unable to tell one beer from another and, I have been told, sometimes cannot tell Coca-Cola from beer. This may be the secret of the Pepsi Challenge that so effectively raised questions about the uniqueness of Coke flavour for the past few years.

3. *Presenter on camera.* Product demonstrations like the Kraft commercials or my early Kit Kat and Aero commercials often do not show people. The verbal message is delivered by a disembodied voice or VO - "voice over picture." When you can see the announcer, it is called "presenter on camera."

The simple presenter-on-camera form of commercial is not commonly used because most creative people shun it. It is "uncreative." Clients are not too fond of it either. "We're paying for creativity, and by God, we want to see creativity." Despite its unpopularity, the presenter-on-camera format is above average in its ability to communicate, to be

The product is the hero of the Kit Kat commercial. The woman, whom you never see, says, "Kit Kat, what a crazy name for a candy bar." Later she asks, "I wonder what the filling is?" and type appears on the screen to answer. It is possible to do a very hard-selling commercial without irritating.

remembered, and to persuade. And it costs less to make a commercial in this style. For that reason it is used effectively by the gadget hucksters - vegetable choppers, kitchen knife sets, and the like. These are powerfully effective commercials that pay their way in immediate results. The hard-sell aura probably taints the technique.

I have wondered why this simple style has selling power. It is, at bottom, the closest you can come to door-to-door Avon lady salesmanship or over-the-counter persuasion. But I feel there are further reasons for the efficiency of this TV sales method compared with commercials where the announcer is invisible. If you wear glasses for short-sightedness, as I do, you have noticed how much more clearly you can *hear* a person speaking when you have your glasses on. There is a certain amount of lip-reading in understanding what people say: "Many run from menace" could be, if you didn't see the lip movement, "Anyone for tennis?" Then, too, there are the overtones of person-to-person communication: the tilt of the head, the candour of the forthright gaze, the body language, the wholesome, truthful *look* of the presenter.

Selection of a presenter takes great care. We were looking for the right characteristics for a presenter to demonstrate a Shell grease to prairie farm viewers. The man we chose had a sincere voice on his audition tape. His photograph looked like the male side of "'Prairie' Gothic." Our crew went to Calgary and filmed the commercial. It was good, convincing. But on first screening I noticed some unusual editing in the product demonstration. A reticent TV producer confessed they had "shot around" the fact that our presenter had only one hand. An authentic farmer, he had lost a hand in a threshing machine.

Why have men been used for so long to talk about detergents and cheese and kitchen gadgets when you would expect a woman to be a better authority? I don't know, but I can make some educated guesses. First, there is tradition. The majority of salesmen, throughout history, have been men. It may simply be easier to accept a male in this traditional role. Second, the top management of most large enterprises is still relentlessly masculine. It may be difficult for the advertising agency (the servants) to urge a female image to an essentially hard-sell executive. Third, in spite of improvement in women's self-perception, it is possible that a lot of women still react to the male as authority. I am sure that the very moment when women presenters produce better sales than men presenters, Lever Brothers, Procter & Gamble, and Colgate-Palmolive will use women presenters exclusively. I have, myself, seen no evidence to suggest that women take advice better from women than from men, or vice versa.

If it exasperates you to have a man tell you a detergent makes clothes white, you can begin to show your displeasure by ignoring that brand. If 10 per cent of the users of any brand were to reject it for a couple of months the advertiser would soon be searching frantically for the cause and would probably change the commercials to a form that restored sales.

When we choose presenters we often consider people who might be accepted as authorities. Bogus authorities, like actors pretending to be druggists, do not work. The consumer quickly sees through it. But a visibly genuine veterinarian can add conviction to a pet food message. A believable nutritionist can sell margarine or canned soup. A noted handyman can help persuade people to buy glue. Best of all, when you find an authority who is also famous, you are in luck. When we were seeking an authority to explain for Shell that driving at slower highway speeds would save gasoline, we used Stephanie Rhys de Perez, who had made a name for herself in car racing. She was a minor celebrity when we started using her. She became a national personality after a few months' exposure in our commercial.

Stephanie Rhys de Perez was a little-known racing driver. She became a national celebrity by appearing in our Shell good mileage commercials. Here she is showing how one can get more miles to the gallon by driving at sixty instead of seventy miles an hour. "It's like getting a free gallon in every tankful." And this was before energy conservation.

Testimonials by ordinary people are well above average in their ability to persuade and to be remembered. The "Candid Camera" type of commercial, where women express their belief in a brand of coffee or detergent, is eternally effective. Testimonials are especially helpful when you are not able to *demonstrate* a product difference - whitening power, deodorant efficiency, flavour.

When a lottery recently went sour in the Atlantic Provinces, our company was called in to sweeten it. A problem with lotteries is that, while some people win, most people lose. Then the most powerful advertising of all, word of mouth, is turned against the lottery. Our solution was simple: we filmed dozens of testimonials from people who had won - not just big prizes but small amounts from a few hundred to a few thousand dollars. The result was spectacular. In a couple of months, people had regained faith in the lottery and were buying tickets as fast as ever.

4. *Celebrity salespersons.* Commercials using well-known celebrities are among the best remembered of all. However, recent measurement techniques show that they are low in ability to persuade people to switch brands. The thinking person's assessment is often, "She's just saying that because she's paid to say it." But *sometimes* the force of personality, the charm, the conviction that makes an actor or an actress able to sell you the role in a drama seems also to help convince you of the merit of a product. Or of their belief in it.

Actors and other celebrities tend to reject working in commercials because it is "commercial." But appearance in a commercial often heightens the familiarity that makes valuable a person who sells personality. A minor talent begins to look like a major one when people see the face and hear the voice frequently repeated on national television. I have never known of a major career to be diminished by appearing in commercials. My creative people have used such people as Vincent Price, June Lockhart, Deborah Kerr, and Johnny Cash to sell products. Luckily for me, they were exceptions in their ability to persuade. All have remained beloved stars, a few dollars richer, and a touch better known. A person appearing in a national TV commercial can be seen by more people in a few weeks than in an entire career on the stage or in films.*

---

* In Canada it is not easy to find celebrities to use in commercials. Most of them go to the States or the U.K. and have done so for generations. Mary Pickford, Walter Pidgeon, Deanna Durbin, and Raymond Massey are a few of the many completely American stars who started life as Canadians. Today, Joni Mitchell, Joyce Davidson, Paul Anka, Rich Little, Christopher Plummer, Hume Cronyn, Jessica Tandy, and Lorne Greene are great American names lost to Canada. We treat our talented people shabbily so now we see them only in *The Sound of Music* and *Battlestar Galactica.*

"One of these Transair seats could be yours for 35% off," says TV personality, Diane Stapley in a television commercial announcing Transair's Summer Bargain Fares. Read on for details.

EFFECTIVE JUNE 15, 1976 Subject to Government approval

FLY 35% OFF

Book two weeks in advance and discover Transair's new Bargain Travel Fares.
They compare favourably with the cost of travelling by train, bus or car.

Bargain Travel Fare seats are in limited supply. First come, first served. Phone now while they last.

We have set aside a limited number of Bargain Travel seats on most flights that save you 35% off the regular fare. All we ask is that you make your booking, and pay for your seat, two weeks or more ahead of time.

Why is Transair offering such a bargain?

Frankly, because there are nearly always a few empty seats. And empty seats cost us money. So to fill them we're offering a bargain price 35% below the regular fare on a "first come, first served" basis.

Remember, the number of Bargain Fare seats is limited. Incidentally, nothing changes but the price! So plan ahead and make your reservations through your Travel Agent—or Transair—as soon as possible.

Compare prices

You'll find Transair's war on prices gives us a clear edge over other airlines...compares fa-vourably with trains and buses...and is, believe it or not lower than travelling by car in many cases. Ask any businessman.

Now read about our other Specials.

Special Family Plan

In some cases, our Family Plan is more econom-ical than our Bargain Fares. And you don't have to book in advance.

The head of the family pays full fare. Spouse and any dependent child, 12 to 21, save 25% each. Children age 2 to 11, travel at half normal adult fare—that's 50% off! You only have to fly together one way to make these savings.

Compare these savings with any other air-line. Call your Travel Agent or Transair today. Then plan that vacation together, or take your family with you on your next business trip.

Savings for Senior Citizens

Transair gives older people a 25% discount. Many other airlines give only 10%. (Summer Bargain Fares save 35%).

These are reserved seats. You're not a stand-by. Transair doesn't like to see Senior Citizens waiting around airports for hours on end.

Half-price Youth Fares

Young people, from 12 to 21, can fly Transair at half price if they're willing to stand by. If they plan to get home for the holidays, we recom-mend they leave before, and return after, the holiday rush.

Save on a Tilden Rent-a-car!

Transair has made arrangements for you to get a Tilden Rent-a-car for $1 off the already low rates on the first day's rental in most Transair cities.

All you have to show the Tilden people is a valid Transair Boarding Pass.

Save this advertisement.

We've described so many Specials in this adver-tisement we suggest you save it for a closer look at your leisure.

And tell your friends about our savings, they may have *missed* seeing the advertisement but don't you let them miss out on all our savings!

For further information about planning your next trip, phone your Travel Agent or call us.

Check these prices to see the kinds of savings available to you by flying Transair Bargain Travel Fares.			
TORONTO TO:	REGULAR FARE	RETURN BARGAIN* FARE	YOU SAVE VS REGULAR FARE
WINNIPEG	$184	$120	$ 64
THUNDER BAY	128	83	45
SAULT STE. MARIE	92	60	32
DRYDEN	170	111	59
YELLOWKNIFE	414	269	145
WHITEHORSE	478	311	167

*PRICES DO NOT INCLUDE FEDERAL AIR TRANSPORTATION TAX

Valid for round trip excursions of 3-30 days on Transair only. Must pick up and pay for your ticket within 10 days of making your reservation and at least 14 days prior to commencement of travel. $15 charge for cancellation or itinerary change after ticket pickup. When you reserve you must specify Transair Bargain Fare. Seats at this fare level are limited and are not available on all flights.

For full details and ask about Transair's Bargain Travel Fares—or call Transair: **869-1700**

Travel Agent and ask about Transair's Bargain Travel Fares—or call Transair: **869-1700**

Think
Transair
First

Another obvious, but powerful headline. Was Diane Stapley an irrelevant celeb-rity? Hardly. Transair flew out of Winnipeg and Diane is a Winnipeg woman. The campaign, on TV and in newspapers, was so successful that Transair was turned from a money-losing airline to a profitable one - whereupon it was bought by a larger airline and we were without a client. The price of success.

When Arthur Godfrey told people to have faith that there really *was* chicken in the Lipton soup mix, they believed. And when he told them to go out and buy Chesterfield cigarettes not by the pack, but by the *carton*, they bought by the carton. Later, he had a lung removed.

All celebrities are not great performers. In the early days of Canadian TV, I wrote commercials for a famous radio personality, Kate Aitken, to sell Good Luck margarine. There was no tape then. We did each commercial live. Kate read her message from a scroll of paper that was rolled from reel to reel by a machine called a Teleprompter. She tended to wave her hands around distractingly, so an impatient young director wrote between the lines of her script, "KEEP HANDS DOWN." Imagine my horror when she said to the nation, "Spread the bread evenly with Good Luck margarine, keep hands down, and add filling."

5. *The slice of life.* In the theatre, a "slice-of-life" drama was utterly (and usually depressingly) realistic. Some ironic soul used the term to describe the unrealistic little playlets that are used to sell detergents, cooking oils, hand lotions, and deodorants. The dramatization is one of the most effective of all formats for communicating with others. You tell a story. A story is always easier to remember, easier to retell: "She says to me, and I says to her" is what makes up most conversations.

The slice-of-life technique of getting ideas across has worked for a couple of thousand years - in the parables of Christ, for example. The "story" way of making things understandable is used to teach the ways of life to students at the Harvard Business School. There, they are called "case studies." These are thinly disguised business cases from real life, such as "How beer sales collapsed when the label was changed."

The slice-of-life commercial uses symbols as stylized as Egyptian hieroglyphics. It is a morality play designed to communicate a maximum of information in a minimum of time. Stereotypes are essential. The women symbolized in the TV detergent parables are stereotypes. They are cut-out paper dolls made to be as acceptable as feasible to a large number of consumers. If these commercials portray women in less than three-dimensional form, remember that they are created mostly by women, that they are usually tested and found persuasive by numbers of prospective women buyers of the product, and that a commercial will not be kept on the air if it is not selling the product.

I believe, by using a little charm and a touch of intelligence, one should be able to make this form of advertising a little more pleasant, a touch less grating. I once made a series of slice-of-life commercials for Softique bath oil. We had discovered that most women think that a bath with soap and water dries up the skin. Barbara Parker invented homely situations - a daughter monopolizing the bathroom, a teen-ager bathing interminably before a date - to show that soaking in the tub need not be drying if accompanied by Softique. The daughter said, after her saturation, "I feel all silky." And the teen-ager's date complained, "she'll dry up like a prune" (a phrase I borrowed from my mother). Each of these became catch phrases. Softique sales rose meteorically. At that time we sold as much Softique for Bristol-Myers in Canada as was sold in the entire United States. The human touch helped make the slice-of-life less stereotyped.

At one time, I determined that we would explore all the likely formats for Ban deodorant. The copywriter and I planned a gamut of styles for testing. We made eleven different test commercials, among them an all-product story extolling Ban's medicated ingredients, a witty cartoon commercial, an amusing funny-girl commercial, and a slice-of-life: "I hate to mention it, Marge, but did you forget your deodorant?" "Oh, I could honestly die." "Here, use my Ban deodorant." (Next day) "Did you have a nice time?" "Oh yes, he took me home - and everything."

We tested all eleven commercials on women to measure which was most persuasive. You can imagine our disgust when the slice-of-life came out miles ahead of the rest. When the commercial was shown on television, Ban sales, which had been in a slump, started a dramatic rise. If they had responded to the witty message, we would have used the witty message. In the long run, consumers get the advertising they deserve.

6. *Music, jingles, sing-and-sell.* Research shows that background music makes commercials less memorable. I suppose that in the brief flash of a thirty-second message, music makes it difficult to hear the words. Often, when a musical background is used, especially in radio, it sounds as if you have two stations on at once.

Music is the red herring of TV advertising. The *artistes* - the musicians, the producers (who usually have nothing else to contribute), the account executives who want to show creativity, and the brand men who want to look contemporary - all of these dilettantes love to dabble in the music end of advertising. They urge the use of the latest musical schtick, ignoring the fact that the young and liberated who favour the newest style are a tiny fraction of the population with very little money to spend. Almost none of them are married or making the buying decisions for the home.

Music is often used to put icing over a half-baked message. It is used to simulate creativity, to mystify clients, to gratify frustrated egos. Hardly a person involved in putting music in commercials has the faintest understanding of the consumer, of her likes, of selling of the product. Music is rarely researched. If it were, most of it would never be used.

Research told us consumers liked the phrase, "Coffee Crisp makes a nice light snack." They did not like "Satisfies without filling" or "A meal in itself" nearly as well. To make the line memorable, I decided to use music. David Ogilvy does not like singing jingles because you cannot understand the words. So I had the performer speak the lines. Coffee Crisp soon became Canada's largest-selling candy bar.

It is a trick of the human mind that words put in rhyme are better remembered than the average "Thirty days hath September . . . ." Combined with a memorable bit of music, a rhymed slogan becomes memorable indeed. This was probably the beginning of the use of music in commercials. Advertisers are often impressed when they hear children at play singing their jingles. Unfortunately, children don't buy soap and the consumer does not sing her way around the supermarket.

The most successful way to use music seems to be in the sing-and-sell format, in which your entire message is in the form of a song, the way the minstrels of medieval times sang the news and history. It seems to work best when your main selling point (product position statement) and the product names are summed up in one of the lines, such as "Coffee Crisp makes a nice light snack," "Noxzema does it naturally," or "To get those things that really count, just say charge it on your Eaton's account."

I said that little research has been done on music. However, there has been continuous market testing on certain melodies for hundreds of years, in folk music. The melodies that have survived are the memorable ones. They are in the consciousnesss of the culture. When creating a musical commercial I almost always start with a piece of folk music or some other work that has survived through popular taste. I mentioned the Pepsi jingle based on "D'ye ken John Peel." A later Pepsi piece, "Now it's Pepsi, for those who think young," was borrowed from the singable "Makin' Whoopee." Lucky Strike had a jingle borrowed from "Little Brown Jug." I wrote my Coffee Crisp commercial to the tune of "Turkey in the Straw" and a Noxzema song related to "Doin' What Comes Naturally."

7. *Lifestyle.* In this type of commercial, the creators hope that if they show vivacious, stylish people using the product, then people who are vivacious and stylish will also use it, *or* people who *would like to be* vivacious and stylish will use it. This attempt to influence people's ways or even to fit in with them is usually indulged in by companies with incredibly large advertising budgets - brewers, soft drink bottlers. Coke is certainly part of the joyful scene with its lovely seasonal messages about little sexpots at the football games, the down-home farm feel, the summer days, Christmas.

Intellectuals rail against these lifestyle commercials that attempt to lure us onward with mirages of the ideal life (some TV commercial producer's ideal, that is, or some copywriter's or some young hopeful brand person's). I do not believe lifestyle commercials are effective, except, perhaps, for advertisers with fantastically large budgets. Even then, I wonder whether the results are not rather a matter of tonnage than of style. Unfortunately, I have never had a client with sufficient money to discover first-hand whether lifestyle commercials are efficient.

Lifestyle messages can help to show the *kind* of people you expect to use your product, such as children for Kool-Aid, youth for colas, Geritol for the very mature.

Some Techniques Used to Dress Up Basic Commercials

Advertising is an art or, better, a craft, like cooking. I have given you the basic recipes - plot lines - for good commercials (and advertisements). It is possible, however, to use exactly the same ingredients in your recipe and turn out a delightful concoction one time and a flop the next. I usually follow tried and true recipes to make advertising. But I have learned a few artful dodges along the way.

Do you remember the White Knight for Ajax detergent and the White Tornado for Ajax liquid cleanser? What were these? Fantasy symbols for the power in the detergents? Memory aids* that stuck to your mind whether you liked it or not? The White Knight sired a genealogy of living symbols. Some surviving offspring: the Man from Glad, the Dove dove. Other examples: the Green Giant** and his Little Sprout, the Pillsbury Dough Boy (Poppin' Fresh), and Del Monte's Mother Nature - all successful, judging by their longevity.

Do these devices work? Memory aids do aid memory. They perform highly in people's recall ability. Some spoilsport researchers say they find that *just because people remember a commercial, this does not mean it has persuaded them to buy.* If anyone tries to persuade you that advertising is a science, remember that the industry's "scientists," the research people, cannot agree whether remembering a commercial will make you more likely to buy or not. They can measure how much you remember, how long you remember - to five decimal places. But they cannot agree that remembering will change your mind.

Some very successful products have been sold with commercials using these memory-aiding devices. But they were also very good *products* and may have enjoyed success simply by having their benefits hammered home with great frequency. Or perhaps they were very good commercials *in spite of* these advertising gimmicks. The memory-aid type of commercial seems to be fading. But don't hold your breath. It may be rediscovered by the next generation of commercial makers.

Less abstract symbols have evolved: the lady storekeeper who recommends Maxwell House coffee, the kindly druggist who recommends Crest toothpaste, the Drano lady plumber, the Maytag non-repairman, Madge the Palmolive manicurist. These symbols, on a more human scale, are as easy to call to mind as your Aunt Mary. They are more useful memory aids because they are earthly beings and can become old friends in your mind.

Montage Commercials

A style of commercial these days (1984) shows you a series of slightly amusing pictures that you are expected to add up to a nice warm feeling for the advertiser. Watching one is like flipping the pages of a Nor-

---

* Memory aids were called "mnemonic devices" by the researchers, a curious illustration of an industry that prides itself on clarity muddying the water. It is pronounced *ne-monic*. Most account executives say *new-monic*.

** Green Giant was originally Le Sur Valley Canning. The name Green Giant first was used on one product only. One can conjecture that the product was canned peas. As I remember, from my early days in my father's market garden, we grew a variety of peas called Green Giant. The Green Giant figure is a powerful memory device and doubtless led the company to adopt it for its entire line.

man Rockwell picture book. (I call these "montage" commercials, following Sergei Eisenstein, the Russian filmmaker who named the many-image technique "montage" in the 1920's.)

Virtually all soft drink commercials show a number of vignettes of summer life - kids in the spray of a fire hydrant, a girl cooling herself with an electric fan, pretty bodies in bikinis, swimming, sports. Bell Telephone shows unrelated bits of emotion to make you feel like calling long distance. The montage technique of using a sequence of evocative images seems to be used when the client or the creative people feel there is little else to say - no product argument, no value message. Its closest relative is the billboard - a form of advertising to "keep your name before the public," a luxury for the average advertiser.

In searching to discover what works in commercials, people like Procter & Gamble, General Foods, Lever Brothers, and many advertising agencies discovered principles that made commercials get their stories over better. One of the basic principles they set down: *use as few changes of scene as possible.* The montage technique defies this principle, an exception that tests the rule. The exceptions are usually very large advertisers. It is like being hit by a whale. Whether it strikes efficiently or not is lost in the great size of the blow.

The montage technique is often copied by smaller advertisers who assume that what the giants do must be right. Canadian advertisers and agencies are often eager to copy the frivolities of the monster advertisers. There has developed, in recent years, a spate of montage messages for candy bars, milk, eggs, nasal sprays, cheese spreads, many of which would be better served by some good sales messages.

Montage commercials are usually not as irritating as others. They are often entertaining. Their low-key, ingratiating quality hides an important negative factor: when you use a performer in your commercial you pay. If the performer speaks, you pay the top rate. You pay according to the number of times you use the commercial and the number of markets where it is shown. If a person is in a non-speaking role, there is another rate. Every extra person in a commercial adds to the cost.* A montage commercial could use a dozen or more people, adding immensely to the cost.

---

* In 1984 an actress appearing in a non-speaking scene in a montage commercial is paid $324.50 union scale for her day of work. If the commercial is used across Canada for thirteen weeks, she is paid $355.02. For each additional thirteen weeks she gets another $355.02. If she is a "principal performer," she earns $324.50 for the day's work, $529.53 for thirteen weeks, and $529.53 for each added thirteen weeks. Two actresses speaking in a slice-of-life would cost $4,236.24 for a year's use. Ten non-speaking performers in a montage commercial used across Canada would cost $14,200.80.

More cost: a montage commercial is photographed in a number of different places - a football field, a city street, a family diningroom. It costs about as much to shoot a scene in one location as it does to shoot an entire commercial in one location. So a montage commercial, in addition to being questionable as to efficiency, can cost many times as much as a commercial with just one scene and a minimum of performers.

Both consumers and advertisers should resent these extra costs. They do not necessarily improve the selling ability of a commercial, yet somewhere, somehow, they have to be paid for. And you know who pays in the end. Perhaps to be free of irritation, to be entertained during the commercial break, you are content to pay the fraction of a cent it costs. And you *are* helping to feed a lot of actors and actresses between plays.

I used montage many years ago for J-Cloths, a product developed by Johnson & Johnson. The product had a variety of uses. I made a commercial with seventy-six scenes illustrating as many uses. Such a barrage of images had never been used in a commercial before. It is one of the more frequently imitated commercial techniques to this day. It was photographed entirely in a studio and the performers appeared in many scenes, to save money.

Johnson & Johnson J-Cloths, the fabulous new fabric with a thousand and

one uses - You can use them as: *Spill wipers,*

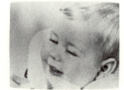

tile wipers,   *Chin wipers, smile wipers,*   *Pane wipers,*

fan wipers,   *Pine wipers,*   *pan wipers,*

Win wipers,

Ben wipers,

Tin wipers,

pen wipers.

Water glasses,

spy glasses,

Looking glasses,

lasses' glasses.

Wall chores,

hall floors,

Lining drawers,

all fours.

Dusting tables,

famous faces,

Famous fables,

famous places.

Polish brass,

clean grates,

98

Wipe slates,   see late lates,   Shine size 8's,

Googahs,   jimcracks,   Thingamabobs

and knick-knacks.   His nib's crib,   dribbles, bib,

Nose,   ears,   porridge,

tears.   Potato chips,   ashtrays,

drips.   Shift teeny,   scarf,

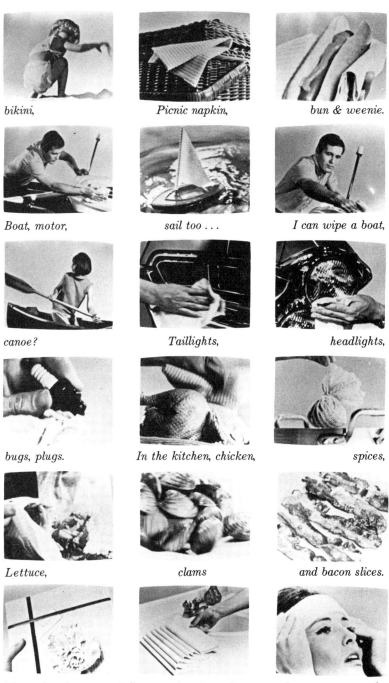

bikini,   Picnic napkin,   bun & weenie.

Boat, motor,   sail too . . .   I can wipe a boat,

canoe?   Taillights,   headlights,

bugs, plugs.   In the kitchen, chicken,   spices,

Lettuce,   clams   and bacon slices.

Wraps for showers and flowers, the nicest Guest towels,   wet towels,

Mess towels,   *pet towels,*   *Nest towels,*

press towels.   *In the boudoir, real gone - Make-up off, make-up on.*

Wipe the stove up, sink and shelf. That's all - now think up more yourself.

J-Cloth* . . . all-purpose towels from Johnson & Johnson.

Food Commercials

In food commercials, the viewer wants a good look at the food, usually close up. Few creative people or film people realize the importance of making food look irresistibly delicious. They fuss with the cutlery, waste time having the mother say, "I want time to spend with my family so I save time in the kitchen with fast, easy (fill in product name here)." They give you a cursory glance at the food as if it were shameful to put the dish before you.

The sound of food is a dimension often missed by commercial makers. They tend to use words or music and forget the *sizzle*. I made

* Trademark of Johnson & Johnson.

a commercial for La Belle Fermiere sausages that starts with a close-up of a frying pan full of sausages and goes closer and closer as a fork tears one in half to show its meaty interior. While the announcer speaks, the spurting and sizzling of the sausages goes on continuously. I like to show this commercial to prospective clients just before lunch. As their mouths water, they are suddenly convinced I am very creative.

To show the crispness of a Kit Kat candy bar I photographed a knife slicing it as a microphone in the picture recorded the crunch. The pour and fizz of a soft drink, the squeak of clean dishes, the perking of coffee add "texture" to the image on the screen.

The first frame of this 'C' Plus commercial and the last frame (not to mention several shots in the middle) show delicious close-ups of the label. When it costs thousands of dollars a second to show a commercial on TV you don't want to leave the viewers in doubt for a single second as to whose commercial they are seeing.

A Good-mannered Commercial Introduces Itself by Name

How often have you seen a commercial that tries to tease you by hiding the name of the product until the end? You say to yourself, "It's a bank," "It's a hamburger chain," "It's long distance," "It's a beer." And then the name is revealed and it's an insurance company.

Research shows that you remember a commercial better if it tells you the name of the product at the beginning. When you receive a letter or a phone call, the first thing you want to know is who is speaking. Only *New Yorker* readers tolerate anonymity until the end of a story. (I don't. I always look to see who wrote the article before I invest time reading it.) When you know that it is McDonald's talking to you, you will look at the commercial with a different frame of mind, probably more active, than if the name is hidden until the end. Every young copywriter starts off life with these "surprise" commercials, hoping to lure the viewer into watching. The viewer, who has seen every trick, simply turns her mind away.

To make a thirty-second commercial today can cost $40,000-$80,000, and I have heard that one commercial introducing a new diet soft drink cost $1 million. To buy time on television can cost hundreds of thousands of dollars. So you see, to make and show a commercial can cost tens of thousands of dollars *a second*. Every second that consumers do not know whose commercial they are seeing is *tens of thousands of dollars down the drain*. Almost every commercial I have ever made, from candy bar to airline, starts with the product or mentions it at the earliest possible moment. These commercials suffered only for being obvious.

How the Product Is Made

Many people in advertising seem to believe that products are a bore, that the consumer should be protected from anything resembling a fact about a product or a service. They create a magical world where window cleaners and candy bars and hair conditioners appear out of nowhere onto supermarket shelves. I have found that people are often interested in how products are made. I took the commercial camera into the Rowntree factory to show how Smarties are moulded, coated with candy, and packaged. Choreographed to music, the Smarties danced on to bigger sales. I showed tomatoes being rushed from field to factory for Campbell, coffee being processed for Yuban, beer being brewed for O'Keefe Blended Ale. I must note that, while consumers were interested and persuaded by these commercials, clients were somehow edgy about them. Perhaps their wives or competitors or boards of directors were not impressed by these sights so familiar to them. Yet, I believe that, especially today, the consumer wants more facts, more reality, more information on how the product is made. Often a plant tour impresses people beyond the wildest hopes of the manufacturer. Their eyes are opened by the degree of cleanliness in food plants, the quality control, testing labs, ingredient quality. Yet the lesson is ignored as TV commercials pretend candy bars are made by

I went into the Rowntree chocolate works to show how Smarties are made and set the commercial to Caribbean music. Kids loved it. Sales leaped up with this astonishingly rational way of selling candies.

elves and corn falls off the cobs into cans. Some daring advertiser will tell it like it is and create a whole new genre.

When I toured the plant where La Belle Fermiere pork sausages were made I was astonished to see that they used the whole pig - excepting the tenderloin - to make sausages. Nearly everyone believes pork sausages are made from odds and ends and are almost entirely lacking in food value. Yet here were sausages being made from the whole pig - roasts, hams, ribs, and all went into the sausages. We tested a list of product ideas using the BIG YES, BIG NO method with this statement among them: "La Belle Fermiere Sausages are made from the whole pig (except the tenderloin)." The result was a curiosity. The idea had the most BIG YES votes and also the most BIG NO votes. The mystery was solved when I looked at the *reasons* for the NO. Women simply did not believe sausages would be made from the whole pig. My solution was obvious - to take groups of women on a tour of the plant and interview them for the commercial camera. Their honest reactions would *convince* viewers that these women had seen with their own eyes La Belle Fermiere sausages being made from the entire pig.

Factual, documentary commercials can be very credible. (The truth is often believable - an idea curiously foreign to advertising people.) In addition, research on consumers suggests that factual messages are *retained* better than "emotional" messages.

The Magic Moment that Changes Your Mind

In all the testing and research done to discover what makes commercials work, I feel we have missed something. Let me illustrate. One evening Helen and I were watching TV when a commercial appeared for a Hunt's tomato sauce with mushroom pieces in it. The commercial did something or other to attract our attention or set the stage, which Helen ignored. Then the sauce poured from the can and you could see the pieces of mushroom. Helen said, "I should try that." It was not the whole commercial that worked. It was the brief instant, a second or two, when the mushroom pieces appeared that made the sale. I saw it happen again with a Chef Boyardee commercial for miniature ravioli. It wasn't the father stealing his son's ravioli that sold Helen. It was the close-up that showed the bite-sized tiny meat pies that got her.

Many of the effective commercials I have made seem to have this magic moment that sells visually and instantly. Milk disappeared from a glass to become an Aero chocolate bar; Aero rose on that little moment to be the top-selling milk chocolate bar in the land. The slicing of the Coffee Crisp bar was a similar moment. Score hairdressing dissolving on the hand, the ladies confusing Good Luck margarine with butter, a Mercedes-Benz dodging safely around a truck, noodles pouring from a soup can - each was an image that epitomized the reason to buy.

Surely the success of commercials depends more on credibility and reality than on the sort of extravagances that we see so often on TV today. I am convinced that a great deal of the elaborate, complex, and costly technique that is being used in commercials could be simplified. More attention to demonstrating the product and explaining its benefits and less to entertainment and vague lifestyles would make advertising better for consumer and marketer alike.

Some commercials turn out to be more annoying than others. I have even heard friends say they believed advertisers actually set out to irritate, with the belief that somehow irritation helps to sell. I have never known an advertising agency person or a manufacturer who *intentionally* irritated prospects. Their commercials may be repetitive, overly simple, loud, tasteless. But they are made in all sincerity to communicate clearly, unequivocally. Sometimes those characteristics annoy. Some advertising people will *defend* harsh commercials by arguing, "Well, they sold the product." I do not believe this is an acceptable answer.

If public reaction is sufficiently angry and loud, and especially if sales suffer, an advertiser will quickly remove a commercial that annoys.

CHAPTER 8

Some Things That Don't Work Too Well on TV

Funny commercials are against the public interest. So are commercials disguised as Busby Berkley musicals, cartoon commercials, commercials that hide the product name till the end, sexy commercials, and probably commercials that have people dressed as pickles.

The reason these and many other commercials are not in the public interest is that they are generally impotent techniques. They cost a lot of money and in the end the consumer pays for these extravagances. While you are chortling over the bumbling husband, ask yourself how much the entertainment contributes to your knowledge of the product. People constantly bedevil me with descriptions of commercials that they believe to be "good advertising." Almost always, the commercials are tricky or funny. I always ask, "What were they advertising?" Nine times out of ten they do not know the name of the product. Try this test yourself next time someone tells you about a terrific commercial. "What were they advertising?"

When a commercial fails to register the product name, the viewer almost always attributes the message to the leading brand. I have been accused of producing a musical for soup, with dancers tapping atop the cans, because friends knew I created Campbell's messages. They erroneously blamed a Heinz extravaganza for the Great American Soup on me. When people raved about the early "bums" commercial for GWG jeans they almost always attributed it to Lee or Levi. (Twenty years ago, I made an amateur film featuring "bums" at the CNE, to the tune of Ravel's "Bolero." Ahead of my time. A friend phoned to ask whether I had made the GWG commercial.)

Anyone in advertising is constantly being advised on what is good advertising:

"I saw a terrific commercial for dog food last night. They had the dogs talking like people, you know, a bull dog talking like Churchill."

"Oh yes? What brand of dog food?"

"Uh ..."

For some reason, advertising writers come all over cute when they have to write a pet food commercial. In research on baby foods and on dog foods, one observes that for both categories the very same product facts are interesting to women. Statements that talk about nutrition, vitamins, minerals, protein, and natural ingredients come out at the top in persuasiveness for baby foods and pet foods. Obviously, you should talk to a dog lover the way you talk to a mother - about the benefit your product offers to the health and happiness of your child or dog. In spite of this obvious consumer attitude, the livingroom eye is filled again and again with Humphrey Bogart cartoon cats, dancing cats, Mae West cats. Mothers want to see real babies in baby food commercials and pet owners are best involved when they see real cats and dogs in pet food commercials.

Intelligent consumers are always tickled by word plays, clever visual stunts like bouncing stomachs or buttocks, literate parodies, and other sugar-coating. Heads of large corporate enterprises are intelligent people. Often, having climbed the executive ladder through knowing how to run an efficient packaging line or an army of salesmen, they have little understanding of the woman who makes the buying decisions. When a senior bank executive says, "Why can't we have something creative like the Alka-Seltzer campaign," or a meatpacker chairman says, "Why don't we do something amusing like those talking dogs," a great many advertising people are happy to go along with it. In fact, a great many of them may not know any better themselves. They mistake entertainment for selling. Most often, the entertainment nullifies the sales effect. This seduction of the intellect brings a lot of ineffective advertising to the tiny screen.

Every national TV spot, it seems, must be gussied up as if it were to be shown at Cannes. Advertising creative people actually hold gala events where they give one another awards for "creativity," a sort of fashion show for commercials. Advertisers naive to the business take misguided pleasure from praise for their agency's creativity. They glow with pride at the awards dinners. If sales sag they seek an even *cleverer* agency. It is astonishing how often an agency wins an award for a commercial and then loses the account.

The people who give and get awards usually have no interest in selling products. They are artists and craftsmen. They know little more about the consumer and her needs than a potato farmer knows about vichyssoise.

Does Humour Work in Advertising?

Humour is the Venus's flytrap of advertising. Sometimes it works. Sometimes it does not.

Humorous advertising is entertaining. It titillates the intellect. Humour reduces the guilt-feelings of writers and producers who feel they are prostituting their "art." Humour civilizes the brute advertising for the intelligent executive. Humour is most admired among civil servants who see it as the essence of good communication because they are so often accused of being humourless. And, since government advertising is not accountable, a frightening amount of it attempts to be *funny*. The nation looks on aghast as TV commercials use comical cartoons to talk about income tax. Should a government clown around?

Humorous commercials are too easy to do. Humour is the second bright idea (sex being the first) of the young copywriter: "Let's show we don't take ourselves too seriously." Also, humorous commercials have a sneak Catch-22: the funnier they are, the sooner they irritate. Who wants to hear the same joke twenty-five times?

Funny commercials have another inherent booby trap - a lot of people have no sense of humour. In research, when we show what we think are funny commercials to consumers, the response is all too often, "Stupid," "Childish." In Toronto, about one in five people come from another country. Our Canadian humour will probably be lost on them. What is amusing in California often makes no sense to the people in Halifax or Kapuskasing. The Newfoundlander's quip can be incomprehensible in the Prairies. How can major advertisers who refuse to risk two executives in the same jet gamble so casually with advertising dollars by using humour?

I do not know what per cent of the population is not amused, or which funny idea will appeal to a wide audience. Comedians sometimes strike an audience that is utterly unresponsive. Or they find they have to discard jokes that they find hilarious but that audiences ignore. There is little research on humour in advertising. Humour is a living thing which, once dissected, dies. It amazes me that advertisers allow so much of their money to be gambled on this intangible. At least every commercial using humour should be tested against a straight version.

When we tested the eleven different commercials for Ban deodorant, two of them were funny, and one of these was a form of cartoon animation. The funny, witty commercial was the second least persuasive. The cartoon commercial was weakest of all. Yet, if we had followed our creative intuition, without testing with consumers, we would have wasted hundreds of thousands of our clients' dollars. (The un-funny slice-of-life, you will remember, worked best of all.) People take their self-image seriously.

There is a kind of advertising that shows a *sense of humour*, a sort of charm, a likable, amusing personality. This kind of commercial is rare, difficult to write well, more difficult to have survive the heavy hands of producers, directors, and actors. The Doyle Dane Bernbach agency does it superbly for Volkswagen and for Polaroid. No cute punch lines, no puns, no jingles.

Cartoons Do Not Sell Well

Cartoons form a subdivision of humour. Animation is used in many ways in advertising. The word "animation" is usually used to identify film action created by photographing a series of drawings to make action - like Tony the Tiger - or a series of carefully adjusted moves of an object or a figure like the Pillsbury Dough Boy. It is also used to show medication swirling through sinuses, beer being blended with ale, skin cream lifting dirt from pores. Where nudity might offend, a drawing of a sexy girl bathing can sell Herbal Essence shampoo. Mother Nature appears in drawings for Del Monte where the real thing might not be so mythical.

Animation is used most usually in cartoon form, like Tom and Jerry or Yogi Bear. Cartoon animation fascinates advertisers. In the early days of TV, animated elves took the dirt right down the drain for Ajax the foaming cleanser and Snap, Crackle, and Pop worked for Kellogg's Rice Krispies. However, research has demonstrated that animated drawings are not as persuasive as real people on television. For some reason this finding was not extended to children. Children watch, with astonishing durability, hours of repetitive cartoon shows. A great many commercials for cereals and other children's products have been promoted with cartoons.

The supposed power of cartoon animation to persuade children has led Canadian governments to ban their use to promote products children choose. I do not believe the subject has been sufficiently studied to justify such a ban. I suspect that a test of the same commercial rendered in drawings and again with real people would show that the real people version would be more powerful. Look at Ronald McDonald. The ban on children's animated advertising has achieved little more than to deny good-paying work to some innocent artisans.

Rules are made to be tested. Procter & Gamble research discovered early that animation was ineffective. I was given a peculiar problem to

The TV commercials for Cheer are, alas, lost to posterity. However, a newspaper version survives, to remind us that every advertising rule has an exception. But be sure you test it with consumers.

solve for Cheer: there was a sort of giveaway war going on among detergents in Canada. Brands were offering tea towels, bathroom towels, drinking glasses, and china packed in with the detergent. P&G decided to fight this trend by arguing in TV commercials that Cheer offered better value for the money than brands that stuffed their packages with premiums.

I decided that the best way to demonstrate the folly of brands containing premiums was to use a gullible husband being suckered into buying them. In my slice-of-life commercial, the naive husband returns from shopping amazed at the beneficence of the soap companies. "Look, towels, glasses, light bulbs. We can furnish the house." The cool wife explains patiently, "They have to leave something out of the package to put those premiums in. It just stands to reason." Then the subdued husband listens as she explains that Cheer also gets clothes cleaner. It seemed to me that the situation would be more palatable if the people were animated drawings rather than real actors. To make the thought of drawn figures attractive to literal-minded Procter & Gamble soldiers, I did not name the commercial "animated version" but "woman's logic version." They bought it. We also made another commercial - a demonstration, a rational comparison with a presenter weighing the detergent from a Cheer package and the smaller amount of detergent in a premium brand. The two commercials were shown in different cities as test markets. The animated version was decisively more effective in selling Cheer.*

Today, I would use live actors for the woman's logic commercial. The slice-of-life commercial is itself a caricature. Consumers accept far more ludicrous characterizations than the witless husband I created.

When I developed Canada's Energy Conservation advertising program there was the problem of giving some very abstract ideas a form you could see and feel. For example, we said that if everyone turned thermostats down a few degrees in the daytime and a few more at night, the country would save millions of barrels of fuel. I turned to Canada's internationally famous National Film Board for help. Here is the commercial we created to demonstrate the fantastic savings possible through individual effort:

What's the difference if I turn my thermostat down? If your thermostat's set at 72° and you turn it down to 68° during the daytime and to 63° at night, you'll save about *four* barrels of fuel oil a year. Did you get that?

72° to 68° daytimes, 63° at night ... save four barrels a year or

---

* Recently I compared notes with some young P&G brand men to see whether they adhered to the same rules. I told them my story and one young man said, "I thought I was about to be the first to try an animated commercial for P&G." Since then, I have noted a Crest commercial using child's drawings.

the heating equivalent in natural gas. If your neighbour turned down, another four barrels saved. The average street could save about eighty barrels. Ontario could save heating fuel to equal 7 million barrels. If all Canada turned thermostats down, in one year we'd save 12 million barrels of fuel oil and 40 billion cubic feet of natural gas. Conservation can make dramatic savings. It all starts with you. If you're not part of the solution, you're part of the problem.

By using the talent of a remarkable animator, Sid Goldsmith, we made an abstract idea overwhelmingly concrete.

In another commercial we showed the lights of the city being turned off as the narrator said:

True, some buildings have to leave some lights on all night. But most big city buildings could set a great example for all Canadians. Downtown Toronto, Montreal, Vancouver. After all, if we don't start conserving energy now, we may not have much choice about it in a few years. Think about it during this moment of darkness brought to you by the Office of Energy Conservation. If you're not part of the solution, you're part of the problem.

  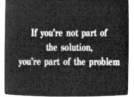

I knew we had a successful commercial when people asked me how we had arranged to have the lights turned off in the city. People believed they were seeing the real thing, and that is convincing.

There is a form of commercial that I have no research experience with. It is the school of advertising that uses real people dressed up as pickles, or ketchup bottles or fruits. They are mercifully few, and that suggests that probably they are ineffective. Perhaps using people dressed up as hamburgers is the frustrated creative people's way of simulating equally ineffective animated drawings. This is not exactly a genre of advertising, but rather a spontaneous appearance, like cretinism, with neither antecedent nor descendant. I imagine it bursts from the head of some budding copywriter who remembers her or his smash hit role costumed as a carrot or a tree stump in the school play. The only excuse I can conceive of for people masquerading as pickles in a TV commercial is to tap some possible latent cannibalism that may lie in our Jungian inheritance.

Emotional Commercials

If humour and laughter are not useful emotions for most products on television, other emotions do not appear to be effective either. In fact, it is surprising, almost unbelievable to most advertising people, that emotional commercials on the whole work below average. (In print, as you will see, emotional advertising works *above* average.) This finding was made in a large study by George Gallup of several hundred commercials and advertisements. The commercials were selected by creative people as examples of "emotional" messages.

Of course, there are commercials that contain powerful amounts of emotion, usually for emotion-charged products or services. Kodak and Polaroid manage, in thirty seconds, to use emotion powerfully with instantaneous heart-grabbers like babies, brides, kisses, dogs. Yet, is it necessary to consume those $10,000 seconds to rouse emotions to sell a magical product like a camera? Is it not more important to show how easily the camera works and what good pictures it takes - and leave the emotion to us? The telephone is another emotional product. Communication is emotional. How much need is there to tell you that you love your parent or child who is accessible by long distance telephone? Yet copywriters keep making commercials to sell you what you already possess instead of telling you how easy and cheap it is to make a long distance call.

When I advertised Pablum, we found that women wanted facts about the product, its nutritional value, its vitamin content. On the assumption that a mother, incipient or recent, would read all we had to say about infant-feeding, Peggy McKeon prepared a very long piece of text. The introductory paragraph said that one's baby tripled in weight during its first year and for that reason Pablum's good nutrition was important. When the time came to render the advertisement into French, Claude Lemenach, the French copywriter, wanted to change this introduction. "I would like to write something to say that you love your baby and appeal to the French women's emotions."

"But Claude," I argued, "if the French women have more emotions than the English women, there is *less* need to use emotion in your text. They will be even *more* interested in reasons why Pablum will be good for their babies if they have more emotion."

Of course, I do not believe there is any difference in the emotions of French or English women. I do not believe, generally, that advertising creates or stimulates emotions in ways that will persuade people to buy. The only emotion I know of that commercials can create quickly is anger, and the only likely effect that has on persuasion is negative. Since most TV commercials seem to act more like outdoor billboards than like a dialogue, it is easy to understand why emotion does not

Pablum Cereals give your baby well-balanced nutrition—with important minerals, vitamins, proteins, carbohydrates and roughage.

A Special Message to New Mothers from Pablum

"Feeding an infant his first solid food shouldn't turn into a battle of wills."
—Eminent Pediatrician

In the first 12 months your baby will triple his weight, eat far more calories for his size than his father, and form his life attitude to eating.

Pablum cereals will give your baby variety to form good food habits and well-balanced nutrition during this fast-growing period.

Pablum was designed by doctors to give babies the right nourishment—nourishment not even supplied by milk. Read on and find out how important Pablum cereals can be to your baby's health and happiness.

DOCTORS START most babies on Pablum* before the fourth month, but it is so easily digested that many babies get their first Pablum when they are only four weeks old!

The first Pablum cereal will be a surprising experience for your baby. He comes ready-trained to suck, to drink. Now, when you feed him his first Pablum, it's as new to him as your first olive.

Expect new reactions. Some babies just ooze their Pablum back out because they don't know what else to do with it. They can't curl their tongues the way you do to swallow. And it takes time to get used to a new taste and new texture. Some babies are just plain mad. They expected milk.

Be patient, be kind, be a mother

Give your baby lots of time to get used to a new food. Forcing or hurrying won't accomplish anything in the long run and, in the short view, causes unhappiness and tears.

Some babies lap up any new food, but every baby has his own way of doing things. If yours refuses cereal that you offer two or three times at a feeding, don't insist. (You might start a contest.) Try again at a later feeding in the day. Be patient. It may take a week, ten days, or even longer to get started on solids.

How to prepare Pablum

A teaspoon is enough for a tiny baby, and make it thin enough to pour. (Thicker for an older baby.)

easily digested. Doctors often start four-week-old babies on any one of these.

For later on

In a few months you can introduce baby to the other varieties. Babies love the taste of Pablum Oatmeal as much as they'll like oatmeal cookies later on. Pablum Protein, you'll find, is especially satisfying for longer periods when a baby is on three meals a day.

Pablum Mixed Cereal is a combination of several grains and, as babies get older, usually turns out to be the favourite. Goodness knows how many months—or years—some children eat Pablum Mixed Cereal.

It's easy to prepare. Pablum is precooked—just add a warm liquid: formula, milk, equal parts of evaporated milk and boiled water, or plain boiled water. A small coffee spoon (demi-tasse) is a good size for food.

Before or after milk?

That's a good question, and it depends on the baby. Try giving Pablum before, at the feeding when he's usually most hungry. If you get too much resistance, try again after the milk. They're not so hungry then, of course, but they're a lot more agreeable.

Happy times with Pablum

Your baby's Pablum times should make him happy and contented and help to develop feelings of love and trust for you. Pediatricians agree that forcing an infant to accept his first solid food can actually be the beginning of a bad eating habit.

Variety sets a life-long pattern

The eating habits formed during your baby's first year set the pattern for life. That's why it's important to give your baby variety right from the start. You help him to build good food habits.

Pablum comes in six varieties. Three to start on. Three for later.

Starter cereals

Pablum Rice, Pablum Barley and Pablum Sobee* Cereal are excellent for starting baby on solids. They mix creamy smooth—never turn lumpy or sticky. They're nourishing and very

But that's all to their good. Pablum cereals have better-balanced nutrition than you get in adult cereals.

Vitamins, minerals, and other nutrients not supplied in milk

Milk is usually regarded as Nature's nearly perfect food—but Pablum Cereal provides vitamins, minerals and other nutrients that your baby does not get in his milk.

Pablum supplies the five most important minerals:

1. Iron Pablum cereal provides iron which is absolutely necessary to keep babies healthy. They need it for their blood. Babies are growing so quickly and increasing their blood supply so rapidly, that they need a ready supply of iron. Milk is not considered a good source.

The iron supply—or the lack of it—is a subject of great interest to doctors concerned with infant nutrition.

Fortunately, Nature looks after a baby's supply temporarily and at birth gives them a reserve of iron. This iron reserve lasts for a few weeks or a few months, depending on many circumstances.

Infants, and adults too, need iron to prevent nutritional anemia.

2. Copper It's an interesting fact that copper is needed so the iron can go to work properly. Iron, without a little copper to go along with it, isn't much use. (We're complicated!) Pablum provides the copper a baby needs.

3. Calcium and 4. Phosphorous There is approximately seven times more calcium and phosphorous in Pablum Cereal than in milk. About half the material in bones is made of these two minerals. And infants grow so fast that they need a good supply.

Your baby's teeth, developing for many months before they actually appear, also depend on calcium and phosphorous for proper growth.

5. Iodine Your baby needs a tiny amount—everybody does. Pablum Cereal gives a baby the iodine he needs.

Vitamins are needed for the many complicated chemical reactions in the body.

Thiamine (Vitamin B_1) and Riboflavin (Vitamin B_2) are supplied in Pablum in the amounts that a baby needs. These two vitamins are part of

If your baby has allergies

Both Pablum Rice and Pablum Sobee Cereals are good for babies who are allergic to wheat. If your baby is suspected of having an allergy, your doctor will probably recommend either of these two.

Any allergy a baby may have to cow's milk will be evident as soon as he is started on regular formula or milk. Babies with this allergy are often fed Sobee Infant Formula*. Pablum Sobee Cereal is the natural progression to solids for these babies. It's a flavourful combination of soya flour and tapioca and is just as nourishing as the other Pablum cereals.

A baby's allergy often does not show up until he starts solid food. If he's allergic to one food only—such as milk or wheat—it's quite easy to avoid that one food.

For a baby allergic to many different foods, feeding can be a problem if a trial and error approach is used in selecting foods. Pablum Sobee Cereal is especially valuable to babies who have allergies to many foods. It is hypoallergenic—it will not cause allergies of any kind.

Some of the allergic reactions that baby might have are eczema, rash, colic, vomiting and diarrhea. Even a slight recurrence of one of these symptoms is distressing to a baby and should be discussed with the doctor.

a Vitamin B group—there are eleven altogether. (Often called the Vitamin B Complex.) Nature usually supplies all of them in the same foods. They are important for good health.

Babies usually get Vitamins A and D (and sometimes C) in vitamin drops recommended by the doctor. Some babies get their Vitamin C in orange juice.

Other food elements Pablum provides are Proteins, Carbohydrates, Fats, Roughage. All are necessary for good health. Here's how they work:

Protein is absolutely essential for growth, for replacing worn-out tissue, and for fighting infectious diseases. A child is born with a "pattern for growing". The first year he grows quickly, and triples in size; the second year his rate of growth is slower. A child must have the proper food, including an adequate amount of protein, if he is to grow the way Nature intended.

Carbohydrates supply energy. Fats supply energy, too, but cannot be the only source. (They are not as easily digested as carbohydrates.)

Your baby uses energy to kick and yawn, squirm and cry. He uses energy for bodily functions. Note Calories are used as the measuring units of energy. When a person eats more Calories than he burns up as energy, the body stores the unused supply as fat. All foods supply energy—some foods are good sources, and some foods are low in Calories.

Roughage is the part of food that cannot be digested but it's used by the body to give proper texture to foods so that the stomach and intestines can function at their best.

Our foods are classified according to the jobs they do best.

1. **Building foods** supply proteins.
2. **Energy foods** supply carbohydrates and fats.
3. **Protective and Regulating foods** supply vitamins, minerals, water and roughage.

Some foods do all three jobs and are especially good. Pablum is one of these foods. That's why Pablum cereals provide well-balanced nutrition. They contain all of the essential food elements.

Pablum's six cereals will give nourishment for your baby's fastest growth

period and variety to help him form good food habits.

You'll find that Pablum makes an important contribution to the healthy development of your baby during that all-important first year.

Historical Note

In the "old" days, babies actually suffered from hunger. They cried for food, but feeding solids that would give them nourishment and satisfy their hunger wasn't started until an infant's teeth came through.

Pablum was the turning point in infant nutrition. It was developed by doctors at the Sick Children's Hospital in Toronto who wanted a nutritious and easily digested food that they could give to infants. Devoted research went into the development of this first infant cereal.

The firm of Mead Johnson produced the cereal commercially. It was called Mead's Cereal. Mothers had to cook it for four hours, but they took the time to do it because babies thrived on it. Fortunately Mr. Mead Johnson's company found a way to precook the cereal—and they renamed it Pablum. (The word Pablum is derived from the Latin word pabulum, meaning food.)

For many years Pablum was the only precooked infant cereal in the world. 　*Reg. T.M.

D-566A

This advertisement prepared by
OGILVY & MATHER (CANADA) LIMITED

You can never tell a mother too much about the health and nutrition of her baby. Although this message is entirely factual, it is charged with emotion because it is read with love.

work in most TV communications. If you have just been laughing up-
roariously at Bob Newhart or you are worried for the safety of someone on *Hill Street Blues*, can you suddenly become all soft and tearful
about Geritol or Jello?

Inside Showbiz Commercials

When you see people dancing in a commercial as though they were in a
fifties Broadway musical you may be seeing a product in trouble.
Yogurt, soup, hamburgers, candies have had their swan dances. Those
commercials often attempt to arouse nostalgia in an audience of TV
generation people who do not understand what the hell is being nostal-
giaized. One of the problems many advertising agency people face is
that they love the entertainment and the movie world. When they
parody a great musical, they expect us all to share the joke. Some of us
have never heard of musicals. Some of us didn't like them. Some of us
do not like people making fun of them. But most important, nobody
ever explained to us the connection between high-kicking chorus girls
and a bowl of soup.

When you see a commercial that obviously has had a lot of money
spent on it for "artistic" reasons, you should start to get mad. For
money wasted on making a commercial, especially an ineffective commercial, is finally paid for by the people who buy the products.

The extra touches that make a commercial look slick are called "production values." Once clients and agencies feel they have conquered
the principles of creating advertising that sells, they start to pay attention to production values. I would caution any advertiser new to the
field to watch out for those words "production values," for they usually
mean "expensive." Those words are in the airline tickets to faraway
places to shoot shampoo scenes in Jamaica and department store commercials in France. Our industry today has arrived at the cynical stage
where the writer and brand man conspire to shoot commercials in ex-
otic places. Oh yes, the brand man and the account executive simply
must attend the making of these commercials in Spain and Sicily and
their airfare, booze, and board is folded into the production cost. Occasionally there is justification - when summer scenes for Canadian car
commercials are needed in mid-winter, for example. But most commercials shot in remote places could be made in a studio.

I once discovered a method called front projection by which stock
shots of faraway places could be photographed with actors in front of
them with the perfect illusion of being there. As far as I know, I am the
only creative person to use the process in Canada to make a TV com-

mercial. (It is frequently used in feature film work.) But it lacks the getaway excuse. The phrase "production values" has many meanings, but mostly it means travel rip-off. The client pays for it in the first step. In the end, the consumer pays.

CHAPTER 9

Newspaper and Magazine Advertising

If the way television advertising pushes itself upon you is a kind of rape, then advertising in print is closer to seduction. In magazines and newspapers, no matter how strident or large an advertisement is, you choose for yourself whether or not to give it your attention. The more aggressively an advertisement telegraphs its intentions with unusual design or colour, the easier it is for you to dismiss it out of the corner of your eye.

Advertising in print, because it need not be designed for the entire world, including those who cannot read at all, can be conceived at a different level from television advertising. Because people consciously choose which magazines and newspapers they want to read, print media select different audiences. You imagine the *Saturday Night* or *Harrowsmith's* constant readers to be somehow unlike those who regularly read *Chatelaine* or *Homemaker's* or *Flare*. The people with attics full of the *National Geographic* are probably not quite the same as those who favour *Toronto Life*.

Advertising in some magazines may be more credible than in newspapers or on TV, at least with the well-educated. *Time* magazine had researchers talk to college graduates who were in business and education. These upper-crusty people profess to read slightly more than they watch TV. Whether they do or not they seem to *believe* what they read in magazines like *Maclean's*, *Time*, and *Reader's Digest* more than messages they get on TV. And they remember the advertising better.

When you know your audience is somewhat literate, your advertising can indulge in appeals to the intellect, like a touch of humour, some

116

verbal gymnastics. Emotional messages work better in print than in
TV. Your reader has time to dwell upon the thought - to be aroused.

How Small Ads Can Grab Your Eye

Print advertising catches interested readers in many ways besides the
particularity of each magazine or newspaper. You are more likely to be
attracted to a large advertisement than to a small advertisement. A
small newspaper ad, say, four inches wide by ten inches deep, will tend
to attract your attention more if you already use the product than it
will reach out for those who have not tried it. Most product sales come
from people who are satisfied with the product, so small-space advertising can help maintain sales.

   Small-space advertising can be used very effectively when one
understands readers' habits. You may have noticed how your own
name or the name of your home town will leap out at you from a newspaper page even though it is hidden away in columns of type. The same
is true when you have a special need (bedwetting, asthma sufferers).
You may wonder at the unpretentious small messages for Preparation
H and other hemorrhoid remedies. If you have had the ill-fortune to
suffer from hemorrhoids, you would find those tiny messages highly interesting and hopeful reading. "Shrinks hemorrhoids without surgery"
is possibly the most electrifying carrot-and-stick promise in all advertising.* Headlines that are baited for very special fish can pull a lot
of readers for small ads: "Mothers," "House Painting," "Computer
Dating," "Lonely?"

   Sometimes, when I do not know who is the prospect for a product or
service, I write ten or twenty small ads appealing to every kind of prospect I can imagine. Then I lump them all together and make a large ad
that adds the extra attraction of size to the special appeal of each small
message. A large newspaper ad, a half-page to a page, will flag down
people who are unacquainted with the product. New products are
quickly introduced to a large number of people by large advertisements. In magazines, colour ads work better than black and white, and
"bleed" pages are better still. A "bleed" page is one where the picture
runs off the edges of the page.

How Pictures Capture Your Attention

The picture in an advertisement is the first thing everyone sees. It is,
about half the time, the only thing you see. The picture should work
even on people who do not read the text, and it should show the prod-

---

* Much better than one writer's attempt at a more picturesque headline:
"Kiss bleeding piles good-bye."

118

uct in use or a result of using the product (or service). The picture helps attract you if you are a likely customer. Also, a picture with a woman in it attracts more women than men, while a picture with a man in it attracts more men. This simple fact, demonstrated repeatedly in readership research, is one of the most misunderstood, even unknown, characteristics of advertising.

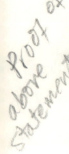

Years ago, Champion spark plugs ran an advertising campaign to remind users that look-alikes do not necessarily perform as well as the real thing. To illustrate the point, they found doubles for people like Clark Gable and Claudette Colbert and printed their pictures alongside the real actors, challenging the reader to pick the real thing. In those days the spark plugs were bought 100 per cent of the time by men. But when Claudette Colbert was used in the comparison pictures, more women read the advertisement than men.

What women look at even more than women is *babies*. They look at pictures of brides, too. And, whatever the product being advertised, from kitchen tile to perfume, if there is a woman in the illustration, women *always* look at the hair style.

Women's obsession with hair fascinates me. I remember my seventy-five-year-old landlady poking nervously at her thinning wisps of hair as if a slight rearrangement would make up for the ragged housecoat or her 200 pounds. "I can't do a thing with it." There are endless hair preparations and advertising for them. I have made advertising for a men's hair preparation, Score, but never for a women's. In my researches I talked with the scientists who create the formulae. "Women do not want really clean hair. If they did, they would use a good soap or detergent to remove all the oil and grease that holds dirt in the hair. They then would add back the oils that have been removed to restore the sheen. What we have to do is make a shampoo that removes *some* of the dirt but leaves an oily residue."

Getting the hair done still seems to be an elixir without equal. The hairdresser is the fairy godmother who changes drudges into princesses. I hope someday to acquire a hair product to advertise. I am convinced that a rational product, presented logically to thinking women, would have a place.*

Reading Habits and Good Advertising Design

Photographs almost always attract your attention better than drawings. It is, of course, childishly logical that, if your attention is arrested by the picture, you will naturally next look *under* the picture, thus

---

* Since these lines were written, our agency has been assigned the task of advertising Tegrin shampoo.

making that the obvious place for the headline. Perhaps because this is so obvious and logical, most advertising creative people, aided and abetted by self-conscious clients, place the headline *anywhere* but under the illustration - over it, beside it, printed on the picture, printed in windows cut into the picture. Readership studies conducted over the past forty years by the Daniel Starch organization, which form the basis for most of my comments about print advertisements, have always shown that when a headline appears beneath the illustration you are more likely to react to it than a headline anywhere else in the advertisement.

This London Life advertisement is specifically for men who plan to marry this year

The Exploding Bag Mystery

We used the classic layout - picture, headline beneath, subheading, text - for London Life. It came to be regarded as "the London Life format" although I have used it dozens of times before and since. When we started to work for Canadian International Paper, I had to invent a new layout for them. The big picture down the side was quite dramatic in newspapers. It became known as the CIP format.

You tend to read advertising in the same manner as you read anything else. Anything that frustrates your normal reading habits tends to cut down your interest in reading. Readership studies, rarely consulted by writers, and never by the layout artists who arrange the components in ads, reveal that the reading of advertisements is a simple, easily understood sequence of human response. For example, if you are like most readers, you like the length of the lines in advertising text to be approximately the same as you are used to in your news-

120

papers and magazines. You prefer the pictures to be square-cornered, like a window. You probably balk at pictures in circles, triangles, or with holes cut in them for type or headlines. You tend to like the pictures, headlines, and type to be arranged in a similar way to the editorial content of a magazine or newspaper. Sometimes a layout artist will have the text printed in white on a black background. For some reason, perhaps because it is the exact reverse of habit, readers find this very difficult. They generally refuse to make the effort to read it. (Appropriately enough, white on black is called "reverse type.")

The Product and the Advertising Design

Here is a fact few advertising people understand: the attention women or men give to an advertisement is most influenced by the product being advertised. People's attention, as you would expect, is closely connected with the things they buy. It is essential that each advertisement quickly proclaims what kind of product it is selling. Men are more prone to read liquor, travel, and automobile advertising. Women read more about food, household products, clothing, cosmetics.

The effect of the product is so powerful that some things, such as women's fashion, motion pictures, and automobiles, can defy every rule of common sense in layout and text and still attract immense attention. Two to three times as many women are likely to read a food or a fashion advertisement as, say, an insurance or a gasoline ad.

How Much Text?

"Nobody will read all that text." "Too many words." This is the most common complaint when you show almost anyone a fact-filled, thorough message telling the consumer everything she wants to know about a product.

Here is what, in my experience, happens to the average advertisement. About 50 per cent of women who read the magazine stop and look at the picture of the average ad. Around 35 per cent read the headline and note the name of the product being advertised. It is true that 90 per cent of the women who flip through *Chatelaine* or *Canadian Living* probably will not read the text in an advertisement. But 10 per cent will read some or all of the text.

Of course, an average is made up of high and low figures. As many as 80 per cent may look at the picture. Some ads are read by very few women. Other ads are read as thoroughly as the articles and stories in the magazine.

It is true that very short text, about the length of the above paragraph, will be read by more women than an advertisement containing as many words as one or two of these pages. Very short text - two, three, or ten words - will be even better read. These research findings mislead many advertisers and copywriters. They reason that, since people appear to read short text more completely than long, their messages should be short. But this is a dangerous line of reasoning in this day when consumers crave facts and information about products. There was a day when the unmentionable could be summed up in two words, "Modess, because ...." Today such products are explained in thorough and candid detail.*

When Mercedes-Benz was just another foreign car, we used long text, sometimes two magazine pages of it, to explain the many engineering features that made it desirable to Canadians. To most advertising people's amazement, men and women devoured the kind of technical, factual information that the Ford and GM agencies withheld, probably on the assumption that most people are too stupid to understand.

If you are thinking of buying a cooking range, you suddenly find every advertisement about ranges intensely interesting. You will read *pages* of information about a range. Pregnant? You read all there is to read about baby foods and diapers. Building a house? Suddenly you develop a voracious taste for facts about insulation, asphalt shingles, and carpets. At times like these you will not argue that the text is too long. In fact, you will complain to yourself that there is not *enough* information.

Long text is especially appropriate for larger purchases. However, my most effective liquor advertising, for Gilbey's gin, used 300 or more words that achieved all-time records in readership *and* in sales increases. I achieved high readership (and won an award) for explanatory ads for Ipana toothpaste with fluoride. For the Milk Board of Ontario, our long messages on nutrition persuaded a measurable number of women to start drinking milk again. I imagine that women would read a great deal of text about hair-care products if it were authoritative and interesting.

It has been my experience that well-conceived advertisements with long text are not only well read but frequently achieve considerably *higher than average* readership. But more important, the people who take the trouble to read facts are *interested* readers. Although 10-per-cent readership may seem rather small, if 10 per cent of the 3,000,000 readers of *Chatelaine* take in your story, you have spoken to 300,000

---

* The liberation of advertising for feminine hygiene products fostered an explosion of product improvements that make life a little more pleasant for women. This is an interesting illustration of one function of advertising, to tell about product improvements: when the conspiracy of silence made it impossible to inform women of the improvements, what was the benefit of improving the product?

122

readers who are interested. To send each of them a letter, allowing 40¢ each for postage and printing, would cost $120,000. (And how many would read it?) A four-colour page in *Chatelaine* costs $19,660 for the English edition. Reaching each person who actually reads your message in *Chatelaine* could cost about 6.5¢. And that ignores the millions more who see the picture, read the headline, and remember the product name.

I try to construct each advertisement to work on all levels at once. Here is an example with long text:

In a Positioning Probe test for Gulf Canada, consumers told us which they preferred from a list of 46 ideas. (The bottom idea was this: "Only a government-owned oil company can be trusted to develop new supplies of oil when they are needed.") One of the ideas consumers liked a lot was, "To encourage energy conservation, Gulf Canada has constructed a 20-storey Calgary office that uses heat from people's bodies and from lights to cut energy use to less than half that used in ordinary buildings." We used this as a basis for the message shown here. The Gulf advertising campaign has changed Canadians' attitudes toward Gulf in Canada. Many see the company as more interested in Canada, more "human," and good for the Canadian economy.

"We decided to apply the best conservation technology in our new Calgary building."

Keith McWalter,
President, Gulf Canada Resources Inc.

The picture is a stopper. About half the readers stop and look and notice who the advertiser is. Whether the picture is large or small, about the same number will stop and look at it. The headline and the subheading give a swift summary of the message for the "hit-and-run" reader - about 30 per cent of readers. Then there is the important-looking text for the interested reader. Even for the non-reader, long text makes it *look* as though you have a worthwhile message. One advertisement in this series was read, by actual measurement in the *Hamilton Spectator*, by 25 per cent of the subscribers - *by one reader in four.*

There is a small caption under the main picture, and more pictures with captions scattered among the text. People *love* to read picture captions. This is probably why copywriters and art directors *refuse* to use them. Yet a caption under a main illustration will be read by 20 per cent - one more chance to mention an interesting fact about the product.

Our factual campaign for Gulf Canada is read by twice as many men as women. We wanted to dramatize the educated intuition that makes people able to divine the presence of oil deep in the rocks of the earth. I uncovered a quotation, "Oil is found in the minds of men," that seemed to say it all. It worked well in consumer testing. When the advertisement appeared, Gulf Canada's personnel manager came to us wringing his hands. Thirteen women who worked at Gulf complained that this was a sexist statement. "Please withdraw that ad. It will offend a lot of women."*

We were re-testing the ads for use in magazines, so we asked the question pointedly of fifty women, "Is there anything sexist in any of these messages?" Not one person commented on the "oil in the minds of men" ad.

This episode illustrates three of my main theses. (1) Don't listen only to your peers - they may be suffering from the Martini Illusion. (2) Use objective research to discover mass response. (3) Of ultimate interest to consumers - a few squawks aimed at the right people could change the course of an advertising campaign.

Does She or Doesn't She React to Slogans?

I have an anti-slogan obsession. I suppose I hate slogans so much because they make advertising look and sound so much like advertising

---

* I wrote Gulf a letter, which I thought they might paraphrase if answers were needed. It said:

About the advertisement headline: "Oil is found in the minds of men."

Obviously, having had good hearing and eyesight these past twenty years it has not escaped me that it is considered improper to suggest in advertising that women and men have special roles. Of course I debated whether or not to use that quotation (which I found in the petroleum industry's book, "Our Petroleum Challenge"). It was apt. For the life of me I could not paraphrase it and come up with the right nuance of meaning - "Oil is found in the minds of *man*" - "Oil is found first in the imagination" - "Oil found in people's minds." They come out sounding like sperm whales.

Jefferson wrote that: "all men are created equal." Fourscore and seven years later, Lincoln repeated it.

Shakespeare, in a similar vein, wrote "What piece of work is man," later used as a lyric on Broadway in *Hair*.

In a way it saddens me to hear about the thirteen knee-jerk comments you've had about the ad. I had thought the whole question of women had reached a new plateau of rationality a little above such unconsidered reactions.

- hence, less credible. One Irish writer I met in New York epitomized my attitude for me: "What is the slogan of the Catholic Church?"

There have been many successful quick statements of the main benefit of a product or service. These have possibly persuaded advertising *copy*writers that *all* advertising should have a catch phrase. *You push the button - we do the rest*: Kodak. This is a complete sales argument in eight words. And still, apparently, it is their basic product development strategy. *More people ride on Goodyear tires than on any other kind*. Hardly catchy, but persuasive. *If it's Borden's, it's got to be good*. I've tried to find a similar set of words that assures quality control as well as this. It is almost impossible.

Slogans are usually so sleek and polished that eventually they slide right through the mind. That is very likely why each of those I have mentioned have been abandoned. Negative adaptation, that sensory trait that turns off the sound of a ticking clock, the refrigerator hum, passing traffic, and airplane sounds, seems also to anaesthetize us to the oft-repeated phrase so that it loses meaning.

I have accidentally used phrases that became slogans. I wrote down "Coffee Crisp makes a nice light snack" among many ideas for that candy bar. Consumers chose it in research. It has been used continuously for more than twenty years. It seems to retain its promise because it is not clever but the sort of thing one might say.

The Canadian Energy Conservation people, being young and therefore experts in advertising, were dying to have a slogan for saving energy. Phrases like "Canada - too good to waste" and such were constantly thrown at me. I was considered an unimaginative advertising person because I resisted these "advertise-y" gimmicks. However, someone suggested the phrase, "If you're not part of the solution, you're part of the problem." It summed up the situation irresistibly, so I used it. I cannot claim to have created it, however. I later discovered that it originated with the Black Panthers.

The Corporate Symbol Complicating Simplicity

Another device that stamps advertising as advertising is the corporate symbol. This is largely a masculine conceit. Sometimes it works. Most often it simply bewilders the consumer. The corporate symbol is the ultimate step along the route that leads from a simple company name or signature through distinctive logo to Rorschach test.

I have been involved in several of these self-indulgent explorations for a symbol. As I looked over corporate symbols I noticed that some of the successful ones use animals or other easily remembered symbols:

Deere, Falconbridge, Bell, Shell. Then there are those daring folks at Eaton's and Sears who say whom they are in plain type without any design frippery.

Many symbols are clever playing with initial letters like the famous CN for Canadian National Railways. But usually the letters are enough (GE, IBM, ITT, GF) to arouse a response. Why do artists believe that making them illegible makes them memorable? Coca-Cola, Ford, Campbell, Johnson & Johnson, and Kleenex seem to have blundered along with their archaic designs. Of course, they touch them up from time to time. But a Coca-Cola sign from twenty years ago still looks pretty familiar. One of my favourites of all is Holiday Inn. Art directors call it one of the most inartistic signs in the history of communication. Probably the only thing that is less artistic is the strain on the face of the Holiday Inn treasurer carrying all that money to the bank.

For some reason, corporate symbols don't get into women's advertising too much. I often wonder if corporate symbols aren't the modern males' way of designing escutcheons for battle. Except they've missed an important point. One of the purposes of flags and crests was to tell one another apart in the heat of the battle. Most of them had lions, eagles, flowers, and things to make them easier to recognize. If you wore a Bank of Commerce symbol to war, you might get executed as an unknown.

Simplicity in Design

My print advertisements are sometimes criticized because, when I follow the logic of readership, they look somewhat like one another. When advertisers complain that their advertisements have a picture at the top, a headline underneath, and the text after that, I explain, "That is the best layout to have your message read. Would you prefer that I give you the second best?" Advertising layout artists and writers say they are not "creative." In fact, my advertisements often turn out to be most unusual because they are the only ones in the newspaper or magazine that have the impact of simplicity.

Sometimes advertisers crave a distinctive look for their advertisements so people will recognize it is their message by its design. Often they achieve an advertisement that looks like an advertisement and warns the reader off.

I do not believe that women recognize the different formats beloved by various advertisers. It is as though the newspapers were required to use a special type style and layout everytime they mentioned the FBI or Raquel Welch, in order that people realize it is the same institution or person being mentioned in each case.

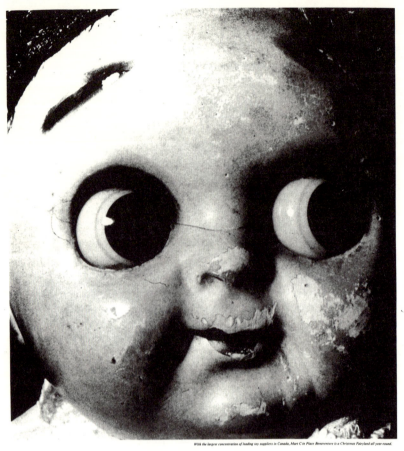

With the largest concentration of leading toy suppliers in Canada, Mart C in Place Bonaventure is a Christmas Fairyland all year-round.

Another success story from Place Bonaventure.

How the Merchandise Mart in Place Bonaventure works for the toy industry...

...not to mention furniture, apparel, floor covering, footwear, houseware and giftware industries.

Mart C in Place Bonaventure is a Christmas Fairyland ... all year-round.

This Christmas-like atmosphere comes from the unbelievable array of toys displayed by the largest concentration of leading toy suppliers in Canada. By congregating in the Mart, they have in effect created a year-round Toyland where wholesale toy buyers come to shop.

Toy buyers can't afford to waste hours going from one end of town to another to see the lines of just two or three toy representatives.

At Place Bonaventure, they can visit many toy suppliers under one roof. Easily. Quickly. Efficiently. That's the Merchandise Mart at work.

An idea that works for all

The Merchandise Mart also works for other industries.

For example, after a shoe buyer has visited Mart A of Place Bonaventure, he has been exposed to practically all the major footwear lines in Canada. Without wasting time. Or gas. Or taxi fares.

The Mart is home to over 600 lines including apparel, giftware, sports equipment, houseware,

hardware, home and office furnishings, floor coverings and many more. We're proud to be Canada's one and only Merchandise Mart!

The Merchandise Mart is only part of the Place Bonaventure story

Last year, for example, over 1,000,000 people visited shows held in the giant Exhibition Hall. And thousands of visitors each day enjoy the pleasure of shopping in our 80 stores and boutiques. You should be one of them.

Place Bonaventure is helping many businesses to grow and prosper. To find out how we can help your company, call 395-2233 for information.

Place Bonaventure

I wrote the headlines; Jackie Grenier wrote the text in this campaign that helped turn Montreal's white elephant into a convention centre. The picture is full of story appeal. The headline tells a complete story. The picture caption, which readers seek out, contains a selling message: With the largest concentration of leading toy suppliers in Canada, Mart C in Place Bonaventure is a Christmas Fairyland all year round.

Women Read, Clip, Hoard Recipes

If there is one certainty in advertising it is that women read recipes. Readership studies always show this. Women clip recipes. They save them, sometimes until the kitchen drawer won't close. They save more recipes than they could use in a lifetime. Some women simply add them to a magpie hoard and rarely see them again. Others, more industrious, file them carefully and *then* rarely see them again. For a sociologist looking for an identifiable difference in the behaviour of the sexes, this is perhaps the greatest.

About twenty years ago, when I was insensitive to women's feelings and when the woman's role was more harshly delineated, I said in a speech to a women's organization:

> Women's obsession with food is desperate. Once the fun of babies is over and the kids become independent organisms, a woman suddenly discovers the only time they do anything but complain is at mealtime. They don't compliment her on clean floors or white washes or doing the washing every week. If a wife and mother is ever going to hear a kind or loving word it's going to be, "Hey, Mom, can I have some more?" or the husband may manage to grunt, "Not bad."

> She aims for the stomach and hopes to hit the heart. Food is her last means of communication. "Have some more cheesecake. Eat, eat."

I have always used recipes wherever possible in food advertising. Recipes help you to rehearse mentally using the chocolate chips or the baking soda. Recipes can make your mouth water. Complicated recipes in advertising, however, are sheer entertainment, starring your product as an ingredient. The best recipes, of course, are those that will be acted upon, thereby encouraging women to *buy* your product and use it. Again and again, you hope. To this end, there are a few simple rules rarely considered by writers, art directors, or dieticians.*

To be used frequently, a recipe should be easy. A can of soup, some pork chops, some chopped onion - that is an almost ideal ingredient list. The chopped onions give the cook a feeling of contributing. (One great cake mix concept was "add a fresh egg and get a better cake." Someone should revive it, changing "better" to "moister.") The advertising recipe should depend on the product for its results. If another product

---

* Dieticians who work with food companies must look upon advertising as an outlet for their frustrated creative efforts. They force brand men and advertising writers to use recipes too complex even for Julia Child. Dieticians are probably very nice at home, but they are often martinets on the job.

How to garnish mixed gin drinks correctly — a helpful lecture from <u>Gilbey's</u>

Some gins have rather strong flavouring. Others are utterly tasteless.
Gilbey's London Dry has the perfect balance for mixed drinks. A <u>dry</u> flavour
that has been the international favourite since 1873. Quite a long time.

The **classic olive** has graced the Martini since its invention. Very proper with the pit. Stuffed olives are acceptable, too. For the rest of the martini, 1 part French vermouth, 6 parts Gilbey's London Dry.

The **lemon twist** has come into fashion as an alternate garnish for martinis. Slice the skin thinly. Twist it *over the drink* so the lemon oils from the skin add their aromatic flavour to the drink.

The **maraschino cherry** makes a nice target at the bottom of a Tom Collins: juice of 1 lime (or ½ lemon), 1 tsp. fruit sugar, 2 oz. Gilbey's London Dry, lots of ice, fill the glass with soda.

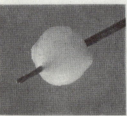

The **pearl onion** is another acceptable garnish for the dry martini (especially when it's *extra* dry). When you have a martini decorated with an onion it's called, for some obscure reason, a Gibson.

A **thin lime slice** trims the Gimlet. Use 4 measures of Gilbey's London Dry Gin, add 1 measure of Rose's Lime Juice Cordial and cracked ice. Then stir gently in the goblet.

Lemon slice sits handsomely on the rim of a gin-and-tonic. Recipe: 2 oz. Gilbey's gin, plenty of ice, and fill up with tonic. Gilbey's London Dry is *especially* compatible with the bittersweet tang of tonic.

Orange slice puts the finishing touch on a Gin Fizz. One part frozen lemonade as it comes from the can, one part Gilbey's London Dry Gin, three cubes of ice. Use a tall tumbler. Fill with ice-cold soda-water. A remarkable thirst-quencher.

Sprig of mint tops a chilly Gin Julep. Formula (since 1860): 1 tbsp. sugar, 1 oz. water, fresh mint. Crush leaves till flavour is extracted. Remove crushed leaves, add 2 oz. Gilbey's London Dry Gin. Fill glass with shaved ice. Top with mint leaves.

Undecorated, try Gilbey's London Dry Gin on the rocks. Smooth and sippable. Try a twist of lemon if you like. It's the *ultimate* dry martini. Always go for the frosted bottle with the diamond-shaped label (above).

Useful recipes, using one's product as a major ingredient, are always interesting - and they send people out to buy the product. Many recipes used in advertising are too complicated or too-seldom used to be of genuine value in increasing product sales. This immensely successful advertisement is a far cry from the one-liner messages favoured by most liquor advertisers who seem to regard their products as boring or their customers as being of limited intelligence.

can be substituted with equally good results, it is not a good advertising recipe, especially if there are cheaper versions of the product around. Here are a few advertising recipe classics:

1. *Eagle Brand Whatchamacallits*
Helen and I spent half an hour rummaging through her recipe file and her drawer full of recipes - she combines both methods of never seeing recipes again - without ever finding this one. It has, however, the important criterion of being easy to remember and pretty difficult to do badly.

$1/2$ 10 oz. tin of Borden's Eagle Brand sweetened condensed milk
About 18 whole graham wafers
Juice of $1/2$ lemon
1 cup shredded coconut
Butter icing flavoured with 1 tsp. lemon rind
8″ × 8″ cake tin

Cover the bottom of the pan with 9 whole wafers.
Mix Eagle Brand, coconut, and lemon juice and spread over bottom layer of wafers. Cover with the second layer of wafers and slather with butter icing flavoured with lemon rind. Refrigerate 24 hours.

About the only complicated thing in that delicious dessert is making the icing. The wafers take up moisture. The whole thing is sinfully delicious. The one weakness of the recipe for advertising purposes is that it is difficult in reading to visualize the results. But once you try it, you are hooked.

I used recipes for Borden's to help sell cheese, milk, KLIM (milk spelled backwards), and Starlac powdered skim milk. If you ever want your family to take in more milk nutrients, use powdered skim milk in your recipes, increasing the amount of powder but not the liquids.

2. *Lipton Onion Dip*
There have been a thousand dips since this one, but none that can compare. It is ten times more addictive than potato chips.

1 envelope Lipton onion soup mix
1 pint (20 oz.) dairy sour cream

Combine Lipton onion soup mix with sour cream.
Cover and refrigerate at least 1 hour. Makes $2^1/2$ cups.

I learned about the soup business working with Lipton. I wrote lines to the effect that Lipton's dried soup "tastes homemade because you cook it yourself right on your own stove. Doesn't get soggy sitting in cans." Later I had to compete with my own advertising approach when

I started to work with Campbell. Lipton onion soup mix was a real "also-ran" until the dip idea came along. Children loved Lipton chicken noodle.

I tried to interest the Lipton people in another folk recipe. (These simple recipe ideas usually arise spontaneously and spread by word of mouth - rarely from dieticians.) Stewing beef and onion soup mix were wrapped in foil and baked. The resulting stew was delicious. We served it in our boardroom to the Lipton people to illustrate what an ideal recipe it was to sell their soup mix. They were unimpressed - "Not of our invention."

3. *Pork Chops and Mushroom Soup*

4-6 pork chops
1 can Campbell's cream of mushroom soup
1 small onion, chopped
Water

Brown chops and onion in frying pan. Add mushroom soup with enough water to thin it. Simmer, stirring sauce and turning chops. This can be for 10 to 20 minutes, depending on how much of a hurry you are in. (Replace the pork chops with chicken parts and you have another easy delicacy.)

When I first started to work with General Foods on Minute Rice, I noticed that they had had a brief upward blip in sales during a period when they had been promoting recipes in which fruit juices were substituted for water in reconstituting the rice. You could use apple juice to make an apple rice to serve with pork or duck, tomato juice for rice to go with hamburger. General Foods resisted this obvious selling strategy for several years. As I write this, I notice that there are television commercials promoting the idea.

4. *Minute Rice à la Sales Blip*

1 cup Minute Rice
1 cup Campbell's consommé

Bring consommé to a boil. Add rice, stir. Remove from heat. It is ready in five minutes. Serve with beef stew, salisbury steak, or hamburger patties.

5. *Frankfurters and Barbecue Sauce*
I have eaten fresh boar in Bad Hamburg, venison in Salisbury, salmon in Largs, deep fried crabs in Venice, steak in Calgary, and smoked pork chops in Rio de Janeiro, but I do not think any of them compares with this.

12 frankfurters, preferably garlic-flavoured
1 can Campbell's tomato soup
1 onion, chopped
2 tbsps. cooking oil
1 heaping tablespoon brown sugar
Juice of ½ lemon
Water

Sauté the onions in oil until transparent and tender but not brown, add lemon juice, brown sugar, soup, water. Simmer until thick. Score the frankfurters diagonally on all sides so the slits open up in the barbecue heat. Brush on the sauce with a pastry brush. Barbecue until the sauce is dark red, maybe black here and there. About 80 per cent of the sauce will drip off into the coals but what remains is pure heaven. (Note: substitute parboiled spare ribs for frankfurters and you have another incomparable delicacy.)

I discovered the recipe in a Wesson Oil ad, of all places. This is *not* an ideal recipe. You can substitute Aylmer tomato soup with good results. I have included it more from a desire to share something wonderful with the rest of mankind. Like a poet.

And for the same reason, I include another folk recipe as an example of one that could *never* be used in advertising because it uses two bitter competitors:

6. *Impossible Pot Roast*

2-4 lbs. blade or other cheap roast
½ pkg. Lipton onion soup mix
½ 10 oz. can Campbell's cream of mushroom soup

Put roast in a roasting dish with a lid. Smear on mushroom soup. Sprinkle on onion soup mix. Put in a slow oven (325°) for about an hour a pound. Some people use the whole can of soup.

The meat comes out tender, the gravy thick and rich. We ration ourselves to once a month for this high-calorie dish.

As money continues to buy less, it is inevitable that the consumer will demand more concrete information about every kind of product. She will seek more facts to help her find the best value. The silly advertising songs and dances and pretty montages on television will not satisfy her craving for product and ingredient knowledge the way advertisements in magazines and newspapers can.

CHAPTER 10

Spelling, Sex, and Subliminals

Advertising in North America is a reflection of the mass culture. I do not accept that advertising creates our culture, as some critics suggest. It is part of it, but it does not play a leading role. For instance, deodorants surely did not create our obsession with being odourless as much as the Puritans did. In Europe, where natural musk is more highly appreciated, deodorants have had heavy going.

I do not know of any case where advertising has introduced a product or service that people did not want. Intelligent consumers object to advertising for pre-sweetened cereals, but the *mass* of mothers appears to be happier with these pacifier foods. The road to oblivion is paved with products that were injected into the culture at the wrong time: the Edsel came when people began rejecting Buick-sized cars. Most failures do not make a big enough crash when they fail to be remembered at all. There was the Fairchild 8MM sound movie camera that rose and fell ten years before Kodak introduced the Ektasound. Freeze-dried baby foods, an excellent idea, were tried and abandoned by Birdseye. I wrote the advertising for the first transparent corn plaster in 1946. Failed. Daisy Diaper Dip, another of my early products, was made redundant by disposable diapers.

Advertising did *not* create the miniskirt, the blue jeans movement, Prohibition, the repeal of Prohibition, the sports car, the split-level house, the condominium, the Pill, Lipton onion dip, the sexual taboos of the fifties, the sexual liberties of the seventies, the hula hoop, jitterbugging or disco or New Wave. In most cases advertising mirrors social changes when they are well-established.

In one well-known case, a product has developed national distribution and billion-dollar sales without any advertising at all. The culture was ready to accept it. That is marijuana in its many forms. If it is eventually legalized, its advertising will very likely follow the style of cigarette and liquor advertising, selling purity of product and brand name. It will be a sad day for racketeers and policemen who have made killings and livings from its suppression.

Good Taste a Matter of Taste

The culture determines taste - good taste and bad taste. Women used to go barechested in public in Bali but not in Toronto, veiled in Iran but not in Montreal. Unshaved armpits are attractive in Portugal, arouse disgust in Winnipeg. In some cultures, like ours, a drunk is funny, in others, revolting. Greek men can embrace and kiss, but don't try it in Calgary.

The Carefree* tampon was a bold idea: not only did it expand to form a more effective retainer than competitors, it was the first in North America to use no applicator. We showed situations where longer protection was desirable. The coupon encouraged sampling. We later discovered that, having no applicator, the Carefree package was much smaller than was needed for ordinary tampons. It was so compact, a full period's tampons could be readily carried in a purse - an added convenience that made the product desirable. I invented the embarrassing moments averted. Jackie Grenier wrote the ads.

Johnson & Johnson introduces CAREFREE* Tampons—
a new concept in sanitary protection.

Sexual and elimination matters have different taboos in different countries. In Germany, an ad for toilet paper will show a woman's bare bottom. In the States, consumer complaints took a Ban commercial off the air because it showed the underarms of nude *statues*. I have had a factual newspaper campaign for Modess cancelled because women did not want their daughters to see such things in print (others said it was about time). I had to take a commercial for Rowntree's Dairy Box Chocolates off the air because women wrote in complaining about the woman presenter's *hair style*. It was a trifle messy. We had to remake the commercial with a more fastidiously coiffed woman.

---

* Trademark of Johnson & Johnson (now known as the o.b. Tampon).

What is good taste? It is a constant see-saw of cut and try. Advertising writers and artists are usually impatient with mass morality and are forever testing the limits of outrage. Advertisers who sell things like toilet cleaners, hemorrhoidal suppositories, and sanitary napkins are perfectly at home with these products and cannot understand why their benefits should be denied the mass audience of television.

I am somewhat Victorian in my own tastes. I do not like looking at toilet-bowl cleaners when I am eating dinner at seven p.m. (Perhaps the Martini Illusion has persuaded advertising people that no civilized family eats before nine.) I wonder when I see messages for hemorrhoidal products on TV. Now there are messages on the tube for condoms. On one hand my inner censor says, "Where will they stop?" On the other, the inner philosopher says that condoms made acceptable are better than unwanted babies and disease. When the culture is ready to accept a behaviour, it ceases to be bad taste.

In Canada in 1984 many women were complaining about feminine hygiene products being advertised on television. If women object to the embarrassment of seeing these messages in the same room with children or friends, or are personally offended, they can help influence the advertiser's thinking by a telephone call or a letter. A few irate consumers can have astonishing impact on a company president.

In a study by Ogilvy & Mather in March, 1979, more than a third of women and men were opposed to hard liquor being advertised on television. Forty-two per cent of women didn't like commercials for feminine douches. TV messages for tampons, sanitary napkins, presweetened cereals, and male genital sprays and powders were opposed by a quarter or more of women. Curiously, advertising for weight-reducing products was unpopular, while only 4 per cent of women disliked messages for toilet-bowl cleaners.

Language and Spelling

While most people do not consider it objectionable to be shown how a brassiere can contain Jane Russell or how a chemical can decongest sinuses, our culture is violent against those who use the language in an unacceptable manner. This is not a new phenomenon. In 1750, Lord Chesterfield wrote to his son, "I must tell you that orthography, in the true sense of the word, is so absolutely necessary for a man of letters, or a gentleman, that one false spelling may fix a ridicule on him for the rest of his life. And I know a man of quality who never recovered the ridicule of having spelled *wholesome* without the 'w'."

The copywriter in Canada is constantly plagued with the problem of Canadian spelling and American spelling. We spell "colour," "vapour," and "cheque" in the English fashion, but "tire" and "curb" the American way. I have received a page-long vilification for spelling "paycheque" in the American manner (paycheck).

I believe advertising has the responsibility of setting an example for the populace in simple, unpretentious use of words and correct structure of sentences and placement of punctuation. I do not favour the two-word sentences and arbitrary punctuation used in much advertising text. Almost a quarter of the population of English-speaking Canada has another language than English as a first tongue: English is tough enough to learn, with its peculiar and illogical spellings and pronunciations (so, sew, sow, sough, plough, tough, rough, through, thorough, you, ewe, yew, knew, sue, etc.), without complicating it with puns, double entendres, and lousy grammar. I believe in a style that avoids fancy words, aims for clarity, and is concrete. My favourite books on writing are *The Art of Plain Talk* by Rudolph Flesch and a slim book on *The Elements of Style* written by William Strunk, Jr., and edited by E. B. White who, in addition to his other works, for a lifetime edited and wrote the "Talk of the Town" in *New Yorker*.

I do not believe in rigid, fixed language usage. Language should be a living thing that adapts to its cultural environment and evolves to suit the needs of the day. But I do not favour hurrying that evolution, especially by linguistically irresponsible and often ignorant groups like the advertising subculture. We in advertising should support and abet the work of the educators.

There is always a blurred boundary between correct and incorrect usage, between imaginative evolution and lazy shorthand. Once I presented an advertising campaign to Goodyear extolling their tires' safety. The headline said, "I think my wife is terrific." The president of Goodyear, a precise lawyer, objected to the word "terrific" because it means "causing terror." "If you mean she is an old meat axe, then it is all right," he said. Having used his needle, he passed the advertisement.

Etymology, the study of historical change in languages, fascinates me. I am amused by discoveries that the words "charity" and "whore" derive from the same root; that the woman's dress style called "redingote" comes from the French word "redingote," which comes from the English "riding coat." (French is not *really* all that inhospitable to other languages. Only Canadian French, where the French word "stop," for instance, was banned from highway signs because it *sounds* like English, has become fanatically against mixture.)

While I endorse selection in the evolution of a useful language, I believe some mutations should be stamped out before they multiply. The Society for the Eradication of the Misuse of "Hopefully" is small but deserving of support. I am worried, also, about "into," as in "into macramé." Some of these fashionable turns of phrase die out. "I've had it" is waning. "Neat" is following "keen" into oblivion, I hope.

The Conflict between "Art" and Plain Communication

In advertising, style embraces illustrations, film editing, music, and most other culture-dictated mannerisms in addition to language use. Here is a memo I sent to the creative department on advertising style:

Saul Steinberg, the artist who draws odd, angular cartoons for a famous magazine, said, in an interview for *Life*:

"I try to avoid temptations like being involved in beauty. I often change a drawing to make it appear more rigid. It seems to me that beauty will detract from the essential idea of drawing. It is like singing instead of speaking words. If I sing, you may not understand what I am saying. I have often made drawings of a fight between man and beauty, beauty (in the sense of a search for beauty) being the enemy. It is not obviously dangerous; it is a siren, and it is a loss of time, at least for me."

In some strange way, Steinberg explains how I feel about TV commercials.

About clarity in TV commercials, I said in another memo to the creators of commercials in the agency that "Clear communication calls for simple settings." I continued:

You have to watch set designers like a hawk. *Many* set designers came up through the art world, not the business world. You have to steel yourself to adopting a "square" position when you deal with them. For Campbell we used Melmac dishes and plastic mats. There's nothing wrong with using Wedgwood china and Dansk place mats, as long as they *look* like Melmac and plastic.

If you don't watch out, set designers will hang abstracts on the wall, use expensive room dividers, pedestal tables, womb chairs. Period furniture is usually okay because most cheap contemporary furniture is copied from period stuff.

Ornate silver, tableware, candelabra, trays, and such usually look more elegant to your viewer than stark stainless steel or plain china patterns. If in doubt, look it up in a mail-order catalogue. Or Birks, if you like. The people who buy from Birks do not necessarily have better taste, just more money.

I once had a writer working with me who had great difficulty putting down a simple, clear statement about a product. Her advertisements were embroidered with silly digressions like "Why is the Mona Lisa smiling?" or "Here are seven things to do with your old iron after you buy Arrow no-iron shirts." I told her, "This is what advertising should be like," and drew a little doodle:

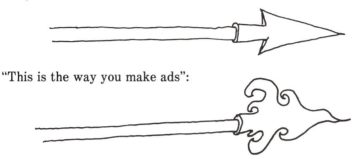

"This is the way you make ads":

Strong Messages without Being Ugly

There is a place for art and decoration, on the walls of homes and museums. Advertising is a craft, whose beauty should be judged by its effectiveness. When form follows function, the results are frequently pleasing. Ogilvy's Hathaway shirt ads, Volkswagen's "lemon" ad, and Young & Rubicam's Johnson & Johnson Band-Aid commercials have a basic aesthetic appeal although they were made to satisfy crass commercial purposes - and did so very well.

I say this about my style of advertising: "I make sledge hammers to break through the walls of indifference. I don't need to paint flowers or butterflies on my sledge hammers to make them work better."

Sex in Advertising

Whenever I am attacked by the angry populace about advertising, it is inevitable that sex rears its head. There is a certain amount of clumsily used sex in advertising. Each new crop of creative people fresh from the chrysalis discovers, along with puns and sans serif type, sex. They confuse things related to procreation with advertising creativity. The consumer often objects. When you consider that a third or more of the populace objects to advertising about feminine hygiene, why are they surprised when a similar proportion objects to sexy advertising?

You can imagine that, in the male-dominated days of advertising in the fifties and sixties, there was a certain reasoning: "Since a woman attracts me, and I want to attract attention to my product, which is boring to me, I'll simply place a woman alongside it and people will look at the woman and therefore at my product." The holes in this reasoning are that (a) more women than men are attracted by pictures of women, sexy or not, and (b) the product - a car, a camera, a forklift truck - is usually more interesting to male readers than any picture of a woman would be. Curiously, you rarely see the reverse, with a lipstick, a computer, or a spaghetti sauce using a "hunk" as the attention-getter. In the fifties' days of masculinity there was an additional motive for using attractive, preferably lightly dressed women in advertising: the art director and the client got to attend the photography session. It smells of old Hollywood but it actually happened.

Some automobile advertising still uses pretty women in a purely decorative way. Considering the sophistication of research by Ford and GM, which must surely tell them that women object to this nonsense, I can only conclude that they use women models to impress their dealers.

Car dealers are mostly men and pretty insensitive men at that. While they usually share the position of richest persons in town, with the local pop bottlers and publishers, they do not usually have a great understanding of public taste. Their ideas on advertising are possibly primitive and of the "sexy girl beside the product" school. Car dealers have immense influence upon car manufacturers. I believe that much advertising for North American cars is made to please car dealers as much as consumers. Mercedes-Benz dealers were continually agitating for advertising that looked more like GM's or Ford's: short text, girls, picture of the car. Mercedes management insisted upon factual text describing the product. Their dealers had to be satisfied with counting their profits.

There *is* a place for sex in advertising - when sex is the consumer benefit being sold. A strip show advertisement would do well to use a picture of the product. The perfume advertisements in *Vogue* seem to suggest there is a reason for smelling nice and Catherine Deneuve was implying *something* when she promoted Chanel No. 5 around Christmas time. Suntan lotions and skin softeners have justice on their side when they show women's bodies in their illustrations.

Marketing Magazine reported a study of the effect of nude female models in advertisements on 141 men. In this experiment, the men remembered as much about ads with no nudes as they did the ads with nudes. More, the men who had "a healthy attitude about nudity in advertising" recalled no more about the advertisements than those who did not. (The report did not state whether a healthy attitude meant nudes were acceptable or abhorrent.)

Male nudes are now being used occasionally. For some inexplicable reason, a nude male has been used to promote a brand of underwear. I am mildly embarrassed and utterly unpersuaded by this irrelevant non-product message. My embarrassment is caused by the puerility of the idea and one more crudity laid at the door of my profession. At least, the underwear should be shown making the male look sexy. Perhaps someone is trying to exploit the fact that most men's underwear is bought by women.

A glorious
rich tan

Val-med

SUNSCREEN

LOTION 65¢

Sex in advertising. Like all youthful copywriters (I had just achieved my major-ity) I was dying to use some sexy stuff. This nude is probably the last to appear in an advertising message for twenty years. However, it was a relevant use of a woman's body because we were selling a suntan lotion.

140

Sex is most often used in advertising by people who know little about the consumers and about advertising. The true reason for me and for you to be annoyed by the sillier uses of sex is that it is an inefficient form of advertising and adds another straw to its cost.

You have probably noticed that gratuitously sexy advertising rarely lasts. My one sortie into the tempting garden of sex was a television commercial for Schweppes. It showed no more than a bottle and two glasses, but the sound track said:

WOMAN: (Softly) Well, here we are. You pour while I put on some music.
MAN: (Turning label to read) Well, whaddya know.
WOMAN: Whaddya know what?
MAN: Schweppes makes a ginger ale.
WOMAN: I buy it all the time, darling.
(Scene changes to bottle and glass on a coffee table, probably beside a sofa.)
WOMAN: You know how the ads say those tiny bubbles last the whole drink through. And sometimes I'm a *very* slow drinker.
(Nothing is spoken for a moment or two. Music only, then the woman speaks huskily.)
WOMAN: Darling.
MAN: (Also huskily) Hmm?
WOMAN: Another nice thing about Schweppes ginger ale.
MAN: (Grunts.) Yeah?
WOMAN: The children love it too.

The main problem with that commercial is that it did not sell any Schweppes ginger ale. In fact, most people thought it was for Schweppes tonic. Too much emphasis on the sexy implications, too little on the product story. The final blow came when the bearded Commander Whitehead came to Canada and saw the commercial on air and ordered that it be discontinued forthwith - "Too sexy." Ruefully, I submit this as an illustration that sex did not sell Schweppes. If Whitehead had not banned the commercial, lack of consumer response would have done so.

Creative people may be tiring of sex. In the eighties, sacrilege is an emerging style with nuns predominating, but priests, monks, ministers, and the devil himself are not spared.

I developed an early interest in sexuality and its influence on behaviour when I studied psychology in university. And one of my avocations is filmmaking. Some of my films explore dream symbolism and mythology, and they inevitably touch on basics like religion and sex. My films have earned more than fifty international awards. So you see, my anti-sex attitude in advertising is more pragmatism than puritanism.

Schweppervescence lasts your whole drink through—even if you are a slow drinker.

Is Schweppes the last bond between English speaking nations?

The sun never sets on Schweppes Tonic Water —the *authentic* tonic mixer. It has a unique, bittersweet flavour; you can tell the difference with your eyes shut. And those famous little bubbles—*Schweppervescence*—last throughout your drink. (Schweppes Dry Ginger Ale and Schweppes Club Soda have Schweppervescence too. They cost no more than ordinary brands).

"Is Schweppes the last bond between English speaking nations?" My slightly sardonic headline was used until a former British Minister of Defence became a senior officer in Schweppes, whereupon it was killed. This ad proved that (a) the tonic water could be sold without Commander Whitehead, and (b) a bottle and glass can be beautiful. The product makes the advertising.

Subliminal Advertising?

In 1954, one Frederick Wertham wrote an astonishing book called *Seduction of the Innocents*, explaining how there were hidden sexual symbols in children's comic books. A crease in a sleeve might look like a reproductive organ. The book had a brief notoriety, then disappeared. In the 1960's someone tried an experiment. The messages "Drink Coca-Cola" and "Hungry? Eat popcorn" were flashed on a movie screen. They reported increases in popcorn and Coca-Cola sales. In spite of these remarkable results, the research has never been repeated or scientifically validated. Nor is there any instance of this miraculous and *cheap* selling method being further used.

While the subject was hot, the Canadian Broadcasting Corporation did a half-hour show on subliminal advertising. At the end, it was revealed that throughout the show a subliminal message to phone CBC's number had been flashed on the screen. Nobody phoned. I watched the show, and as far as I was concerned subliminal advertising was buried.*

Then a public relations man named Wilson Brian Key conceived one of the cleverer illusions of modern times. He dredged up the idea of hidden sex symbols and combined it with the sinister thought of subliminal messages to create the theory that advertisers sell products through hidden sexual messages. He applied the term "subliminal" to the kinds of perfectly obvious images we see when we look at clouds or ink blots (when, in fact, "subliminal" means "below the threshold of perception," a very short exposure or at very low intensity).

His book, *Subliminal Seduction*, is an adroit pastiche of psychoanalytical and marketing jargon presented as *facts*. It is very well put together and has the advantage that nobody can consult his authorities, Jung, Freud, and Marshall McLuhan now dead, and the advertising and marketing wise men unnamed. Feeding on the ferocious public mistrust of business and an emerging mysticism, in the seventies Key's book was a runaway success.

In a supreme test of academic freedom, Key was allowed to teach his theory to students at the University of Western Ontario, much to the

---

* However, there is still today a section regarding subliminal devices in advertising in the Canadian Broadcasting Act. A publication of the Institute of Canadian Advertising, *The Source, The Authoritative Guide to Advertising and the Law*, states: "No station or network operator shall knowingly broadcast any advertising material that makes use of any subliminal device. 'Subliminal' device means a technical device that is used to convey or attempt to convey a message to a person by means of images or sounds of very brief duration or by any other means without that person . . . being aware of the substance of the message being conveyed or attempted to be conveyed."

chagrin of Labatt's Breweries, one of the university's major supporters. I note that, while he cites experiments using students ("The Gilbey ad made me horny"), he does not name the university. It has been a surprising lesson to me that students lapped up this anti-authority nonsense without question. One would have thought that scholarly, sceptical young people in the era that said, "Never trust anyone over thirty," would examine these ideas presented by a smooth talker then well into his forties. Almost any statement in his book would collapse under the simplest rational examination. Yet his house of Rorschach cards held up. Even today apparently intelligent people dig me about "subliminal advertising."

While I was chairman of Ogilvy & Mather in Canada, I appeared on a television show with Key where he was flogging his book. Before the show, I phoned the president of Gilbey's and asked how he liked the suggestion that the word "Sex" was spelled out in his ice cubes. He laughed and said it was unfortunate they hadn't discovered this secret years earlier. I talked with Bryna Feingold, the creative person who had made an ad for Chivas that Key suggested held a "subliminal" dog hidden in the shadows of some crumpled wrapping paper. She said she couldn't see a dog, but maybe there was a gorilla. And she gave me the original photographic transparency that was used to make the advertisement.

When we met in the make-up room before the show, Key revealed that he had worked with one of Ogilvy & Mather's clients as a public relations man in Puerto Rico. As far as I know, he has no further claim to academic or literary authority.

On the air he spoke about the hidden sex in *Playboy* magazine, though he did not explain the need here for hidden sexual symbols. When I showed him the Chivas transparency he insisted that it "must have been retouched." He said that Rembrandt had hidden the letters spelling sex in his paintings. I asked him, "How do you spell 'sex' in Dutch?" I didn't know the answer, but it stopped him.*

There are still people around who wholly accept Key's argument, as there are those who believe in the Bermuda Triangle myth, "The Chariot of the Gods," Pyramid Power, and horoscopes. I recall a Catch-22 conversation with a young intellectual - a social scientist, woman, and communist - who believed the subliminal proposition implicitly. I argued that I had been practising advertising at a high level for major advertisers all of my working life and had never encountered a case of anyone attempting to use hidden sexual symbols in advertising. She in-

---

* One ponders why Rembrandt should use the word in his paintings when he had produced works showing the act quite explicitly.

sisted that I must have been using sex *unconsciously* because it was there.

I have worked in advertising all of my adult life. I have spent days with the Viennese motivational market researcher, Ernest Dichter; I have worked with the greats of Young & Rubicam and Ogilvy & Mather; I have worked with, trained, and learned from many of the worthwhile advertising people in Canada. Never, in any conversation, act, or deed, did any one of these people even mention the possibility of subliminal advertising. Perhaps I dignify it too much by spending this much space on it.

In the Rorschach test, people see all kinds of things in the ink blots: animals, fish, insects, birds, faces. And, where very obvious, penises and vaginas. Should a subject see sexual meanings in every ink blot, the analyst would be alerted that there was something awry in that person's psyche. If you see an excess of sexual symbols in advertising words and illustrations, ask not for whom the symbols sound, they may be trying to tell *you* something.

Key's book was innocent enough. It caused little harm other than to irritate the occasional advertising man at church meetings and bazaars. It is, however, an interesting study in social hysteria, the kind that, in more malicious forms, burns Salem witches, jails Canadian citizens of Japanese descent, forms lynch mobs, and worse.

CHAPTER 11

Advertising:
A Mirror of the Culture

Advertising, used effectively and honestly, has a place in the North American culture. Advertising is part of the economic ecology that has made Canada and the United States the most prosperous, most comfortable countries in the world.

However, this book is not meant to defend advertising. Its purpose is to tell you how advertising works so you can think about it rationally rather than emotionally. When you realize that the methods and motives of advertising are no more complex or subtle than those of any other craft, you are better armed to understand it.

The complaints against advertising, like detergents, come in many sizes. A frequent complaint against television advertising is that "the sound is too loud."* Broadcasting technicians who control the strength of the signal going out to your TV aerial tell me that they don't allow a higher level of sound for commercials than for the shows. They are sensitive to viewer complaints. In fact, as opposed to commercials, television shows chat away at normal conversational pace, some words lost, some emphasized, probably using fewer words per minute than are used in a commercial. Then along comes the commercial that costs the advertiser thousands of dollars for *every word*; it is only human to

---

* Passage from Canadian Broadcasting Corporation (CBC) regulations: "Commercial messages *must* be produced in such a way as to avoid an impression of excessive loudness and be presented at a pace that can be comfortably followed. (A maximum of 150 words per minute is a standard that is frequently followed.)"

get in as many selling points as time will allow, with each word enunciated with strong emphasis and equal volume. The result, in contrast with the show, is certain to be an impression of loudness.

Where music is used in a commercial, it is often of the rousing, quick-paced kind. There are only thirty seconds in which to establish the melody, sing the words, and send you away humming to the supermarket. An ordinary non-commercial musical number will just be warming up after thirty seconds.

Government Watchdogs

I have often said, "About all you can believe in the media is the advertising." It is very nearly impossible to exaggerate, let alone tell straight untruths in television. Consumers seem to be totally unaware of the bodyguard of rules and laws that surround everything that is shown on television.

For instance, any drug product advertised in television must pass through government departments that check every word against medical evidence, tests on rats, chemical analysis. Procter & Gamble had to do tests of their Crest fluoride toothpaste on hundreds of children for *five years* before they were allowed to claim that it could reduce cavities. When I tried to write advertising for Ipana toothpaste, which had a very similar fluoride compound added, we were not allowed to make claims for cavity prevention because the tests had not been carried out for Ipana. Procter & Gamble has always had a very simple approach to marketing. They invest in research and development to produce the best product possible before they spend on distributing and advertising. Tide detergent was powerfully advertised, but not until P&G was certain the product would wash clothes better than anything on the market. The money P&G invested in Crest research was staggering. But they gained a five-year advantage over their competitors.

When I wrote advertising for Campbell's soups, I discovered through research that women were interested in the fact that, contrary to popular belief, the canned soups were good sources of vitamins. The client and I visited the Department of National Health and Welfare to get permission to say in our commercials that tomato soup was "a good source of Vitamin A." Not "excellent," for that would put us into a different classification. The regulations are that carefully defined. It is one more example of the twentieth-century misunderstanding - while the general public believes advertisers have licence to say whatever they believe will sell a product, advertisers themselves are tangled in an undergrowth of regulations that fill books.

In Canada we are not allowed to say that a premium is *free* if it is necessary to buy a product to obtain the premium. One must say "At no extra cost." Similarly, you cannot claim that the vitamins in milk will do you any good because those vitamins are in milk naturally. We once wrote that a diamond we were offering as a Shell promotion was "multifaceted" (having many facets). It turned out that "multifaceted" is a technical description of a certain kind of diamond. Shell was sued. Shell won.

Once, we ran a contest for Shell in which buyers of Shell products received numbered promotion pieces. In order to shorten the time of the contest, the numbers were selected in advance by a computer. Our promotion piece said on it, "You may already have won a prize." On the logic that most of the people receiving the promotion piece could not have won because the winning numbers had already been selected, legal action was mounted against Shell. I had just taken over as president of Ogilvy & Mather. My first presidential experience was a visit from the Royal Canadian Mounted Police. They seized our files and Shell's at the same moment. The fact that they were in plain clothes, and one of the pair that walked into my office was a woman, did not make the experience any less alarming. I felt like a hunted man for many days. My lawyer told me the first thing the investigators go for is your desk blotter because that is where big shots hide their notes of price fixing and other illegal deals.

In Canada, a food or drug commercial has to run a gauntlet of approvals to get on TV. For example, a television commercial for a soft drink has to have a stamp of approval from the Department of National Health and Welfare, the Canadian Radio and Television Commission (Commercial Clearance Department), Advisory Standards Council (ASC), and, depending on which stations it appears on, may also need approval by the Telecaster Committee and CBC Commercial Clearance Department. In the United States commercials are scrutinized by the networks to protect themselves from claims of false advertising or poor taste. And nervous advertisers have every commercial examined by lawyers because consumer complaints can beget nasty lawsuits. If one's commercial is to appear on Canada's government-owned television network, it must receive *their* O.K., which is often withheld if you even mention another product in any way. In a gasoline commercial we had to blot out the word "Ford" that none of us had noticed on the rocker panel of a test car.

The Honesty-in-advertising Fad

There was a period in the sixties and seventies when the exciting news about advertising perfidy was dishonesty. Because of the problems of photographing delicate things like ice cream, mashed potatoes were substituted. Resentful union members would report any photographic aid to create trouble: perhaps the most notorious was the marbles-in-the-soup "scandal," one of the silliest in advertising history. Probably because it comes as close to motherhood as a corporation can, Campbell must watch its step as it walks among the thistles of public opinion. People remember "marbles in the soup" to this day, although the event occurred over twenty-five years ago. It is a physical fact that the ingredients in soup, being heavier than water, sink to the bottom. A bowl of vegetable soup, after it has been posed and lighted in the studio and the vegetables have settled, looks more like a bowl of dishwater than soup. When you eat soup, you dig in with your spoon. You dredge up the ingredients to cool them. It is constantly in motion so you see the ingredients. To make the soup look like soup, a photographer hit upon the ingenious idea of putting clear glass marbles in the bowl so that some of the ingredients would be held in view to make the soup look the way it does when you eat it. Although this is perhaps less devious than wearing a Cross-Your-Heart bra or colouring your hair, the public was stunned. "Marbles in the soup" became, quite unjustifiably, an example of the deceptive cunning of advertising people. (The problem never entered my life for I always photographed the soup, in motion, being poured or spooned.)

The witch hunt about honesty in advertising grew to such fanatical dimensions that an Ogilvy creative person wryly wondered whether the model who wore an eyepatch in the Hathaway shirt ads would have to have an eye removed.

I do not know where one draws the line. I have used wide-angle lenses to show more of a room, slow motion to give soup, soft drinks, and Metrecal a more realistic look as they pour. How do you place four bottles of Schweppes *exactly* in a row before a running camera? You simply line them up and have someone *lift them away* one at a time. Then you print the film in reverse and the hand places the bottles exactly in place.

When I first made commercials about energy conservation for the government, the Canadian Broadcasting Corporation refused to run them because there was no real proof that there was a shortage of energy. When we demonstrated that a lightweight automobile used less gasoline than a heavy automobile, we had to supply bushels of documentation.

In Canada and the United States, the advertising business itself has censoring groups that make sure the industry does not foul its own nest. I was admonished not to use the phrase "Drink Wink" if the commercial was to appear at a time when children might see it for fear they might take this as a command.

Common Complaint:
"All products are alike."

After a company like Procter & Gamble has spent large research funds developing a product, other manufacturers will attempt to sell you a copy of the product. Ipana with fluoride was an example. A failure. I have had little experience with these freeloading products. There may be successes among them. But in the end, the product makes the advertising. If the product offers no benefit, the advertising for it will eventually fail. A "me-too" brand soon differentiates itself from the product it imitates - usually by lowering price, offering premiums, or improving the formula.

Canada's first detergent. Sales skyrocketed as wartime shortages cut off supplies of soap powders like Rinso and Oxydol. Dipfoam was harsh and it didn't foam. Sales collapsed when other detergents were introduced by P&G, Colgate, and Lever. I was a boy-copywriter - about twenty-one - when I created this hyperbolic campaign.

I suppose the most common complaints about advertising and marketing are aimed at soap companies: "All detergents are alike. Why do we need to have so many?" Detergents are not alike. When I worked with Procter & Gamble, Tide was the most effective detergent you could buy for getting clothes clean. P&G has always tried to maintain this leadership. The brand for which I wrote advertising was Cheer. I started to write for New Blue Cheer when it was white. During the white days, the Tide formula was used for Cheer. P&G had introduced its own "me-too" brand. And Cheer was not very successful. Then it was decided to use a different fluorescor in Cheer. Fluorescors are used in detergents to make clothes look whiter and brighter. You have seen these dyes used to make stage costumes glow in the dark - under ultra-violet light. There is a lot of ultra-violet light in sunlight, so when your clothes are well-coated in the fluorescor from your detergent they gleam whiter and brighter in the sunlight. Until Cheer came along, the fluorescors had a yellowish cast. Cheer's was more blueish. It gave an impression of greater whiteness and Cheer became a success.

At one time I compared the washing abilities of different detergents with their prices and found that you get pretty well what you pay for. People who argue that we don't need that variety of choices do not consider that some women demand the very best whitening and cleaning power available and they are willing to pay for it. Others are quite content with cheap but adequate cleaning and whitening. It is an individual choice. Yet, a trait of some public-spirited people is to believe that their own needs or perceptions are those that should prevail. They would limit products to, say, one size, probably the giant economy size, without considering that many people's cash flow does not make it practical to make large purchases of manufactured products, that the giant bottle of Coke won't fit all refrigerator shelves, or that the ketchup in the huge bargain bottle will turn black before it is all gone in some households.

When there are too many brands of spaghetti sauce or too many sizes of headache tablets, natural selection tends to eliminate the misfits. The choices of the consumer decide, in the end, whether Tide is too expensive for the cleaning job it does or whether individual servings of breakfast cereals make sense in a family with individual tastes. Advertising is shaped by the products and the needs they fill; it does not create the variety of products. But advertising helps give a wide variety of choices to the consumer.

Advertising for Social Benefit

Most advertising agencies contribute their time and talent to selling beneficial concepts like The United Way, fund-raising campaigns for universities, promoting UNICEF cards. And the power of advertising is there to be used to promote other ideas in the public interest. In the mid-seventies I was able to demonstrate that the power of advertising can work to *curb* appetites as powerfully as it can whet them. Working with the Department of Energy, Mines and Resources, I developed an advertising approach to energy conservation that changed attitudes - the way people thought about electricity, fuel oil, gasoline. Researchers asked Canadians about their energy habits before the advertising ran and again after.

There was a measurable change in attitudes toward using energy. After a year of conservation advertising, people were more inclined to drive slower, to turn off lights, to lower thermostats. Ontario experienced a reduction in demand for electrical power that surprised the energy predictors. Of course, news stories and events, too, heightened awareness of energy problems. But advertising, at even a low level, helped reduce demand. The Canadian government spent less to introduce the idea of conservation than was spent to introduce Skippy peanut butter to Canadians. Canada's energy conservation advertising program was named the best in the world at an international conference on conservation held in Paris and was used as a model for the United States advertising program (eventually to sink along with President Carter).

The Morality of Advertising in Politics

I feel most uncomfortable with my craft of advertising when attempts are made to use it in politics. The results do not bother me so much as the intent. Eisenhower complained of being sold like a tube of toothpaste at the nomination convention. The techniques were naive and hucksterish and I doubt they had anything to do with his nomination or election. But advertising people have been entering political campaigns increasingly. Adroit television commercials bombard the public at each election. In Canadian politics, they seem to have had little effect upon the voting attitudes. It is, perhaps, foolish to expect people to respond to these slick interruptions to television entertainment that they have been trained to discount for so many years. It is especially quaint to believe that these clever, slanted messages are perceived by voters as having no connection with the news, with personal experience, with a neighbour's opinions, all of which are a hundred times more influential on one's attitudes.

In Canada the calibre of people who have been involved in political advertising is not always of the highest. Politicians choose strange promoters. The rewards are immense for an advertising agency that helps elect a man to power. The government is Canada's largest advertiser. When a political campaign is manipulated as cleverly as was Nixon's (cf. *The Selling of the President*), I worry. He used show business people and advertising people to create a person the American public wanted, a person quite unlike the real Nixon. Advertising, like firearms, can be dangerous in the wrong hands.

I have no concern with someone advising a politician on how to look good on television. A good husband would do as much for his wife before a PTA appearance. Nor do I feel it is wrong to fix up the grammar or to clarify a politician's message. If advertising people are employed to make a politician's wording more dramatic, I do not wince. Not everyone is a natural spellbinder like Lincoln or Sir John A. Macdonald. Many advertising people are intensely political themselves.

Some have entered politics with moderate success. Both Churchill and Roosevelt have been quoted as saying they might, in other circumstances, have gone into advertising. (I can't imagine either of them kowtowing to a brand person as even the mightiest in advertising must, at times.)

I would work with the right politician if I were asked. I would put to work all my beliefs in research in discovering what the voter needs and wants. I would use my penchant for facts and credibility. I would pay special attention to the fact that half the voters are women. Above all I would demonstrate as unpretentiously as possible that *the product makes the advertising.*

Advertising to Children: Wicked or Benign?

It appears that advertising to children will be sufficiently surrounded by bans and laws that it will cease to be an issue in a few years - the rules and regulations about advertising to children issued by Canada's governments are many. All of this, however, does not say that advertising will not affect children. In a report by TVOntario, the province's government-supported educational network, is this comment: "... in 17% of our homes young children control the home sets, with another 42% sharing the decision-making well into evening hours, with the *peak viewing hour for children under twelve coming about 8 p.m.*, tapering off gradually, with some children watching with their parents even up to midnight."

If you are a parent, you have probably been enraged by your child's insistence on an advertised brand in the supermarket. If your authority over your child is not strong you will likely end up buying some of these products whether or not you consider them beneficial or nutritious. In this satiated society, some mothers are secretly grateful to TV for persuading their children to eat something. I am personally repelled by advertising that overpromises (lies) to children: the products simply do not and cannot deliver what the commercials lead children to expect. Advertising for certain toys has exploited the vivid imaginations of small children in ways that are quite ruthless. The child's mind is sufficiently imaginative without the need to exaggerate or romanticize. I can remember when I was four, weeping with longing for the toys displayed in Eaton's mail-order catalogue.

It is questionable, in fact, whether advertising needs to be tailored especially for children to be effective. I have often suspected that cartoon advertising designed for small children is less persuasive than more "hard-sell" commercials might be. I remember when my own children were obsessed with the desire for a Slinky, a coiled spring whose only asset was that it made a compelling TV commercial. (I wanted one myself.)

Parents blame television advertising for influencing their children when they might ask themselves whether they help the children to evaluate television. The TVOntario report said children learn more effectively when they view programs with teachers and parents. Surely this is true for commercials as well.

Children and Advertising Aimed at Adults

I learned a remarkable lesson about advertising to children when I created commercials for Rowntree chocolates. We assumed that Aero milk chocolate bars were bought and eaten mostly by adults. Our research was done on adults. The statement that adults found most persuasive about Aero milk chocolate was that each bar contained "the nourishment of almost three ounces of milk." Our commercials showed a glass containing 2.8 ounces of milk, which then mysteriously disappeared and reappeared as an Aero milk chocolate bar. Sales shot upward and Aero for a time became the top-selling milk chocolate bar in Canada. Then we did what we should have done in the first place. We sent researchers out to discover who was really eating Rowntree products. We found that most Aero chocolate bars were bought and eaten by *children*. We had been creating rational, factual, almost hard-sell adult commercials and showing them at night to reach adults. We ended up with a runaway success with a product bought mostly by children.

This magic moment - not more than three seconds - showed that Aero milk chocolate really contained milk nourishment. People thought I was too obvious in this approach to advertising chocolate bars, but commercials containing this scene made Aero the top-selling milk chocolate bar in the land. Aimed at adults, and broadcast in adult shows, it sold Aero to children.

I have been criticized for influencing children to buy Campbell's soups. I never did show anything but the cans, the ingredients, and bowls of soup. Children were affected by these factual commercials even while I aimed for the mothers. It seems that *all* advertising is observed, assessed, and reacted to by children. It is little wonder to me that we have grown a generation of sceptics when, from the moment children can comprehend, we allow them to see product messages that turn out to be plain lies as far as their everyday experience demonstrates. By the time a child is eight years old, the mind automatically censors and discounts. Scepticism reaches its peak in young people from twelve to fifteen years of age. Television advertising suffers from a sort of "psychological inflation." Each statement is devalued by lack of credibility. Because television has such vivid impact, the resulting scepticism and cynicism is intense. We have created a generation that questions *everything*.

And yet, all is not lost. I have sufficient faith in the resiliency and intelligence of the human race to believe that in another generation we will have absorbed television. It will take its place among other great cultural earthquakes like the inventions of cuneiform writing and the printing press - earthshaking for a moment, then part of life. This is not a defence of advertising and selling, but an attempt to put it in some kind of perspective among the countless other things human beings consider to be worth doing.

The laws and rules that govern what can be said in advertising are often maddening to advertising people. It is not surprising that when bureaucrats question every attempt at facts or comparison, copywriters prefer to write an innocuous jingle or joke. The consumer should be more aware of the ways she is protected against deceit in advertising by government, the networks, and the advertising industry itself. She should learn how far she can trust advertising, for advertising that is believed is more efficient than advertising that is mistrusted. Perhaps the governments themselves owe it to the public to explain - even using paid advertising - how consumers are protected.*

Hoist with My Own Advertising Petard

They say that sales people are the easiest to sell.

There was a toy doll that was advertised on television. She was called the "Betsy Wetsy," and she brought home the problem to me.

---

* For sources that will supply detailed information on consumer protection in advertising and for a summary of the various rules and regulations, see the Appendix.

You probably remember what Betsy Wetsy did. My four-year-old daughter Susan saw Betsy Wetsy on television. She asked us for a Betsy Wetsy with non-committal results. But that hardly mattered to Susan. She wrote a letter to Santa Claus asking for a Betsy Wetsy.* Helen refused to yield to the pressures of television advertising. We both told little Sue that there would be no Betsy Wetsy under the tree. We hardened our hearts and repeatedly told her that she could expect no Betsy Wetsy. But she *had* asked Santa Claus. She had unshakeable faith that Santa would bring her a Betsy Wetsy because she had asked him.

Somewhere along the countdown to Christmas my resolve cracked. I went to each toy department and they were *sold out* of Betsy Wetsies. Finally, Eaton's discovered that they had *one* Betsy Wetsy left. I bought the last Betsy Wetsy in Toronto. Helen was not pleased with me. On Christmas Eve, the stockings were hung over the living-room fireplace. Relatives were sleeping in our bed so Helen and I put a mattress on the living-room floor for the night. At five a.m. the children were up to see what might have appeared in the stockings. The Betsy Wetsy was sticking out of Susan's stocking. Susan hugged the doll, and with tears streaming down her face she held it to my face, "See, I *told* you he'd bring it, Daddy. I *told* you."

Well, we should have *told* her there was no Santa Claus in the first place. I certainly do not blame the advertising for my weakness any more than my mother might have blamed the Eaton's catalogue for making me crave a Sandy Andy.

Earning a living by selling things and influencing attitudes as I do, my assessment of my craft goes from an abysmal low, as it did when I read *The Selling of the President 1968* by Joe McGinniss and found I knew one of the people involved, to moderate heights, as when I introduced a worthwhile product like Johnson & Johnson's J-Cloths, helped people lose weight with Metrecal, or helped make Canadians become a little less wasteful in their use of energy.

In this weighing of my craft, I ask myself, "Is selling Betsy Wetsy entirely wrong?" Besides bringing inordinate joy to a little girl for a few dripping moments, I have also contributed a mite to the saleslady's salary in Eaton's store. I have helped create a moment of work for the person at the plastic machine moulding the Betsy Wetsy, and another portion of piecework for the skilled worker boring the hole for the wet to come out and for the checker who makes sure the hole is well and truly bored. Then there is the chainsaw operator who felled the tree and the hundreds of other men and women who helped turn the wood into cardboard to make the box that Betsy Wetsy came in. What of the

---

* How often was my experience repeated with Cabbage Patch Dolls?

printer and the inkmaker who emblazoned the box with Betsy Wetsy's picture; the trucker who hauled her to the store; the credit department who industriously totted up my purchase, billed me at the end of the month, and charged me 18 per cent interest when I was tardy in paying; the advertising people who made the commercial demonstrating Betsy Wetsy's incontinence; the television station whose employees are paid in part from the proceeds of Betsy Wetsy's advertising and the show people whose show carried the Betsy Wetsy commercial? And so on.

One might comment that Betsy Wetsy, and indeed the commercializing of Christmas itself, might easily be done away with and none the worse. Perhaps so. But most of life not directly involved with basic nutrients, procreation, and avoiding freezing to death is, to some degree, in the same category as Betsy Wetsy, from the automatic gear shift to the Sistine Chapel ceiling. Not essential, but they do improve the quality of life.

What You Can Do About Advertising

If you have read this far, you now know more about advertising than most consumers do (and perhaps more than many advertising people). You know that the two major shapers of advertising are the product and the consumer, and that most consumers are women. You know that advertising people tend to get *between* the product and the consumer. They assume the consumer is too simple-minded to accept the plain facts about detergents or candy bars. Too many advertising artisans are convinced that the consumer is persuaded to purchase by pretty songs and amusing pictures rather than by the product's true benefits. You now know that advertising people are inclined to be more interested in how beautiful or witty or daring or sexy a commercial or an advertisement is than they are in what it says. Form becomes more important than content. You know that the advertising subculture has evolved a priesthood of research Jesuits, creative medicine men, and production cantors who have persuaded themselves and their clients that their magic is the right magic.

I have said several times that an advertising message is not likely to survive if it does not sell the product or change attitudes. So why do we continue to hear incomprehensible jingles and see irrelevant pictures and learn so little about the product? Why does this inefficient advertising persist? If I say the consumer helps shape the advertising, why does advertising continue to be made that women say insults their intelligence? Why do silly, frothy, factless commercials survive? Why do women in commercials keep on acting like cretins? Why do people still think commercials are too loud?

Between the lines in the research, in conversation with consumers when I have spoken to education groups, church groups, conservation groups, women's clubs, and in listening to women discuss products and advertising in group interviews, I sense impatience with today's advertising. The dissatisfaction is there but women are not yet mad enough to do anything about it. They tolerate the clowns because they entertain. Even though we are struggling out of a major recession, North American consumers are still too wealthy and complacent to demand more concrete information in their advertising. The advertising industry reached a peak of efficiency, of no-nonsense style and lean pragmatism, in the years of the 1929-39 depression. As the realities of inflation and belt-tightening continue - probably for years - women may again find that, as the purchasing agents for the family unit, they have to spend cautiously. Then they will reject the frivolous and demand information. The time is close.

The Power of the Consumer

Considering the proportion of spending controlled by the consumer-women in the North American economy, they have the power to make advertising and, in fact, most industry change their ways. Women who buy for house and family do not recognize the immense power they possess. Their slightest frown can make industry leaders jump. Twelve letters from women made Johnson & Johnson abandon our factual campaign about sanitary napkins. Half a dozen complaints about a hairdo killed a Rowntree commercial. Women's objections may modify the TV advertising of personal hygiene products. Outraged boycotts in the Nixon era brought down the price of meat. Women brought in slacks and miniskirts despite the clothing industry. The power is there.

In the buoyant years after World War II the North American family had money and was eager to spend it. Manufacturers sold all they could make of refrigerators, ball-point pens, instant coffees, and frozen foods. They often *ran out of* canned tomato soup, convertibles, Betsy Wetsies, and electric can openers. Products often became shoddier, and complaints were usually handled peremptorily. Over the years the North American consumer lost faith in her rights as a consumer. "Who would pay attention to me?"

But the consumer lost her power by failing to exercise it often enough. She tolerated toasters that failed to pop up and seams that parted because it was easier to throw the thing away and buy another one. She came to expect a phalanx of secretaries and complaint departments and lawyers to dismiss her complaint and simply sighed when she found debris in the pop bottle, hated a soap commercial, or was aggravated by the computer-written letter. The after-war era of plenty created a lethargic consumer who didn't bother to demand and manufacturers who forgot who was the boss.

Marshalling the Might of Women Consumers

When I directed the advertising for Canada's Energy Conservation program, I proposed that most of the conservation goals could be reached by changing women's attitudes toward energy use. As part of the program, I asked a well-known woman to speak out about conservation. She demurred, saying (a) she did not wish to be identified with the government in charge, and (b) what could one little person like her do anyhow?

Following our conversation, I wrote her a letter detailing the ways women as consumers could affect energy consumption. The letter ended:

> If women who work in the home, who make buying decisions, followed even a few of the practices outlined in this rambling note, if they would just start to change their own attitudes and the attitudes of those around them, they could eliminate *nuclear plants, refineries, hydro lines, dam sites.*
>
> It's almost all possible if attitudes can be changed.
>
> And little, helpless you have the power to change attitudes.

Ms. X did not reply to my letter, so one woman's decision ever so slightly retarded Canada's energy conservation effort.

Despite Ms. X, consumer attitudes did change (partly as a result of our energy conservation advertising). Many people chose to drive smaller cars, lower thermostat settings, and take other conservation measures. These actions have indeed stopped the building of many new nuclear plants in Canada, caused the closing of refineries, and lowered our wasteful use of fuel, bringing our country a little closer to energy self-sufficiency. Small decisions, almost unnoticeable actions, made by the millions of consumers can have great positive impact upon the economy.

The Letter to the President

Perhaps most women do not realize the electrifying effect a letter to the president can create. You suspect, of course, that he will not see it or not act upon it in person. In many cases you may be right. But you can be certain that your letter will be given the kind of attention by the president's interceptors as if the president *had* received it. The interception is often intensely motivated: there is always the chance the president might receive a letter that gets the quality-control people or the shipping department or the production people in trouble, and then there is hell to pay. A letter to the company, a letter to the "complaints department," a letter to the sales department can easily be side-tracked, but a letter to the president *cannot* be ignored. If you are feeling really malicious and indignant, you can write to one of the government or industry bodies listed in the back of this book.

When I first realized the power of letters to the president, having had advertising campaigns killed on account of them, I advised a couple of friends to try it. When the mast of a styrofoam sailboat broke loose, a woman friend wrote to the president of Eaton's at my urging. Eaton's solved the problem quickly. When an American Motors automobile was delivered with the steering wheel upside down, an acquaintance, at my suggestion, wrote the president saying he wondered whether the wheel was wrong or perhaps the wheel was right and the *car* was upside down. He received instant attention and a phone call from the public relations officer.

Businessmen, now that the seller's market is gone, are coming to realize the value of the satisfied customer and the terrible havoc that can be caused by the dissatisfied customer. The unhappy consumer talks a hundred times more often and is believed far more than the satisfied one. Intelligent business heads heed your complaints. They want not only to stop you from bad-mouthing their products but would like to convert you to a gratified and, they hope, talkative customer.

Young & Rubicam once ran an advertisement that said, "We create the world's second best advertising," going on to say that the best advertising was the personal recommendation of a product by a friend. The reverse is true, too: is there anything that will cool your interest in a cook stove, a brand of frozen peas, or a skin cream faster than the slightest hint against it from someone you know? Businesses know this. They act swiftly to stop the spark from becoming a fire. In addition, your complaint may be valuable to a business head. It could reveal a weakness in their products or their inspection systems. No industry wants Nader headlines. Your letter will get action. Newspapers and television have used consumer complaint features with success in recent years, making manufacturers jump and correct errors.

Complaints Can Improve Advertising

Women's complaints about products can help improve them. The consumerwoman can also act to bring about the kind of advertising she wants. It is no use wailing that "commercials insult my intelligence." It is pointless to yell at poor advertising agency servants like me that the commercials are too loud or that they do not give enough hard information. You will bring no changes in the portrayal of women by haranguing brand people or sales managers. (They cannot concede that they are wrong.) You have to get the attention of the company's top person. And you have to make a specific complaint about a specific advertisement or commercial. If you hate the music, say so. If the product is misrepresented, say so. If you have seen the commercial too often, say so. If your friends agree with you, urge them to say so as well. *By letter, to the president.* When the president queries a commercial, everybody jumps. If you are so fortunate as to have the same complaint about a commercial as the president's *wife*, your voice will be as the voice of ten. A fashion commercial with sexy overtones for Eaton's department stores was cancelled instantly upon a complaint from one of the senior ladies of the family. It had cost, according to rumour, more than $100,000. Unfortunately, Eaton's advertising department was not as wise about sex in advertising as you are, having read Chapter 10. Or as the Eaton lady, following her instincts.

Collective Power to Change the World

We owe it to one another to complain when we don't like products or advertising. Complaints help improve products and advertising. We make the laws of natural selection work by assailing the inefficient. But these are minor skirmishes so far. They are tiny seismic blips that hint at the earthquaking power that could be liberated if women decided to act in concert.

Aristophanes' sardonic play, *Lysistrata*, tells how the women of Athens and Sparta, led by the heroine Lysistrata, ended a war between their states by denying their men any conjugal contact until they stopped fighting.

I suggest that if the consumers of the North America want to halt objectionable advertising, they can do so simply by withholding favours, by refusing to buy the product or service that is advertised badly. They can do the same about products or services that do not please them. If women could ever get themselves together they would wield power that could alter the behaviour of most industries, international corporations, supermarket chains, TV networks, and other insensitive giants. It could be called the Lysistrata Movement.

Let me demonstrate the possibilities of such a movement with a real situation where consumers acted more or less similarly, though unconscious of their common behaviour. I witnessed this event first-hand because I was working on an advertising campaign explaining to Canadians why the pulp and paper industry needed better tax breaks and a healthier profit. The whole of Canada depends heavily upon the newspaper industry for jobs and prosperity. About one job in ten is connected with the forest.

For some reason, in 1981 and 1982 consumers in the United States and Canada decided to spend less money in stores. The stores and many manufacturers consequently had less money to spend in newspaper advertising. The newspapers therefore were not as thick and needed less paper, and that slowed papermaking. Thus, the act of buying just a little less at your favourite boutique or supermarket made Canada's largest manufacturing industry tremble. The men and women who operate titanic tree-harvesting machines, the miners who mine the iron ore to make the forest industry's bulldozers, the railroad workers who haul the paper to the cities, the executives in their Lear jets, the women who sew the surveyors' tents - all of their jobs in some small way hang on your decision whether or not to buy that new jumpsuit.

The effect the weather sometimes has on business demonstrates the fantastic accumulated influence of small, almost inconsequential decisions. When it is too hot to move or, more often, when it is uncomfortably cold and blustery out and you decide to put off your shopping excursion, you're taking part in a movement that makes storekeepers and manufacturers weep. Cold weather cuts down on beer sales but improves the sale of soup because you and millions of other people tend to drink less beer and enjoy more soup when it is cold. Most people decide whether to buy a new bathing suit or make do with last year's before July 1. If the weather in May and June is cold and unpromising, the effect on the bathing suit industry is appalling. The reverse holds for winter coats. If the weather is not really cold before the turn of the year, a lot of people will decide last year's will do. There were three years in a row when, in Ontario, the weather remained warm until after Christmas. Several companies who specialized in overcoats went bankrupt. A warm November-December has depressing results on Christmas sales. People just don't feel Christmasy when there is no winter chill in the air.

A rainy day may deter only one person in ten from shopping. A warm November Wednesday might make five mothers in a hundred decide to stay home to rake leaves instead of buying Cabbage Patch dolls and Yodas for their children's Christmas stockings. They are not big decisions. Most people are hardly aware of withholding their money, yet these small actions multiplied by tens of thousands can make the difference between profit and loss, can cripple companies. I cite these cases of numbers of consumers deciding to do the same thing at the same time having unexpected impact on industries to show that, even with a little orchestration, consumerwomen could have a great influence on what is made, bought, and sold and how it is advertised.

If consumerwomen detest a certain TV commercial or believe it to be too silly or trivial to remain on the air, it would disappear quickly if even a small percentage simply stopped buying the product. And almost instantly if they also wrote letters to the president.

I hesitate to expand too far the potential of the Lysistrata Movement. With even a modest concerted effort something like a meatless Friday could make meat prices tumble and increase the consumption of Valium among cattlemen and meatpackers. The fishing industry would prosper. One can imagine women breaking the thrall of the fashion industry by common consent to wear the same clothes to two cocktail parties in a row. Or families overcoming their reliance on McDonald's and Colonel Sanders by learning how to make hamburgers and fried chicken at home.

Suppose, by some turn of fate, consumers decided to band together to affect the way things are, what might be their strongest weapon? What about that old black magic that you know so well - advertising? If you could somehow coax each thoughtful consumerwoman, with fund-raising advertisements, say, to contribute about 25¢ a week, you could have the largest advertising budget in Canada - bigger than Procter & Gamble or General Foods, or Nabisco, bigger even than the Canadian government, the largest advertising spender in Canada.

In the meantime, please do not chew me out because advertisements insult your intelligence. Do not chastise me because your children demand sugar-coated corn flakes. Do not point fingers at me for sexy ads, for incomprehensible jingles, for factless commercials. You get the advertising you deserve. If you don't like it, don't buy the product, don't buy the service, complain to the top dog. It will disappear, like magic.

Appendix:

Advertising Rules and Regulations*

compiled by Micheline Tremblay

All television commercials are subject to the federal and provincial laws, industry codes, and guidelines as outlined in the Institute of Canadian Advertising's *The Source, The Authoritative Guide to Advertising and the Law*. The regulations have special approval procedures for the advertising (television, radio, and print) of alcoholic beverages, food and drugs, and feminine hygiene products and for children's advertising.

Every commercial message broadcast by a television station licensed to broadcast in Canada requires clearance and/or registration by the Canadian Radio-Television and Telecommunications Commission (CRTC) before it can be shown. (The only exceptions: commercial messages produced by a licensee for use only on its own station(s), public service announcements, and station and network promotions of their programming.)

While all the various government regulatory and clearance bodies listed below have guidelines for acceptance, they exercise a wide degree of discretion in the interpretation of the guidelines.

---

* For the most part, this appendix has been condensed from Institute of Canadian Advertising, *The Source, The Authoritative Guide to Advertising and the Law*.

164

Canadian Radio-Television and Telecommunications Commission

This is a government regulatory body with which all TV commercials must be registered before they may be broadcast in Canada. The CRTC requires compliance with industry codes and standards as part of the terms on which broadcasting licenses are granted.

The CRTC's regulations have detailed provisions concerning approval procedures for children's advertising and the advertising of alcoholic beverages (wine, beer, liquor), food and drugs, and feminine hygiene products. Radio or TV commercials and any print advertisements promoting these products can only run after they have been reviewed by either the Advertising Standards Council (ASC) or the Department of National Health and Welfare, have script or copy approval by the CRTC, and bear a registration number assigned by the CRTC.

In reviewing commercial scripts, the CRTC may ask for the deletion or substitution of certain words and expressions or may reject complete scripts it deems not to be in good taste.

Any changes whatsoever made to commercial scripts or storyboards must go through the entire approval procedures again - by the CRTC and any other mandatory clearance body. For further information contact:

Advertising Co-ordinator
Commercial Clearance Department
CRTC
Ottawa K1A 0N2
Phone: (613) 997-0313

Advertising Standards Council

The ASC was established by the Advertising Advisory Board (AAB). It is a self-regulating advisory body to the Canadian advertising industry and an approval body for feminine hygiene and children's advertising.

Children's Advertising. The CRTC controls this type of advertising by requiring all broadcast stations, as part of their licensing commitment, to adhere to the Broadcast Code for Advertising to Children. This code is enforced by the ASC.

Feminine Hygiene Products. A television code of standards for the advertising of these products has been created by the Canadian Association of Broadcasters (CAB) in co-operation with advertisers, their advertising agencies, the Telecaster Committee, and the ASC, which administers the code.

For further information on the role of the ASC, contact one of the following offices:

Advertising Standards Council
1240 Bay Street, Suite 302
Toronto, Ontario M5R 2A7
Phone: (416) 961-6311

Le Conseil des Normes de la Publicité
1499 rue de Bleury, Suite 200
Montréal, Québec H3A 2H5
Phone: (514) 849-5086

Advertising Standards Council, B.C. Region
P.O. Box 3005
Vancouver, B.C. V6B 3X5

Alberta Advertising Standards Council, Calgary
P.O. Box 2990
Calgary, Alberta

Alberta Advertising Standards Council, Edmonton
P.O. Box 9009
Postal Station "E"
Edmonton, Alberta T5P 4K1

Advertising Standards Council, Saskatchewan
P.O. Box 1322
Regina, Saskatchewan S4P 3B8

Advertising Standards Council, Manitoba
P.O. Box 1001
Winnipeg, Manitoba R3C 2W3

Advertising Standards Council, Atlantic Region
P.O. Box 394
Station "M"
Halifax, Nova Scotia B3J 2P8

The ASC does not clear commercials for use in Quebec. There, all commercials directed to children must receive approval from the Quebec Advisory Committee to ensure compliance with Articles 248 and 249 of Bill 72. For information regarding advertising to children in Quebec, contact:

Government of Quebec
Consumer Protection Bureau
5199 Sherbrooke St. E., Suite 2360
Montreal, Quebec H1T 3X1
Phone: (514) 256-5061

Canadian Broadcasting Corporation

All advertising for broadcast on CBC facilities must meet the requirements of the Criminal Code, CRTC Broadcast Regulations, and CBC Commercial Acceptance Policy. For CBC Commercial Acceptance guidelines and procedures, contact:

(French Services)
Société Radio-Canada
1400 est boul. Dorchester
P.O. 6000
Montreal, Quebec
Phone: (514) 285-3211

(English Services)
Supervisor of English Services, CBC
Commercial Acceptance Dept.
135 Maitland Street
Toronto, Ontario
Phone: (416) 925-3311

Telecaster Committee of Canada

Formed by private broadcasters in 1972 as a voluntary self-regulating committee, this is a non-profit organization funded by the following member stations and networks: CFCF-TV, Montreal: CFTM-TV, Montreal; CFCM-TV, Quebec City; CKMI-TV, Quebec City; CFCN-TV, Calgary; CFPL-TV, London; CITV, Edmonton; CITY-TV, Toronto; CJOH-TV, Ottawa; CKCO-TV, Kitchener; CKSH-TV, Sherbrooke; CKTM-TV, Trois-Rivières; CKVR-TV, Barrie; CKY-TV, Winnipeg; Atlantic Television System; British Columbia Television; CTV Television Network; Global Television Network.

The primary function of the Telecaster Committee is to ensure each commercial aired on these stations and networks complies with Committee guidelines and meets the requirements of the CRTC Broadcast Regulations. For further information on Committee guidelines, contact:

(English Services)
Co-ordinator, Telecaster Committee of Canada
c/o CTV Television Network
42 Charles St. E., 8th Floor
Toronto, Ontario M4Y 1T5
Phone: (416) 928-6045

(French Services)
French Co-ordinator
P.O. Box 170, Station "C"
1600 Blvd. de Maisonneuve East
Room A-492
Montréal H2L 4P6
Phone: (514) 598-2899

Advertising Advisory Board

This is a body that protects interests of advertising agencies, advertisers, the media, and consumer groups in Canada.

Sex-Role Stereotyping: Special Advisory Committee. In 1979, a special government task force originally formed by the CRTC was restructured to examine more in-depth "how women are addressed and portrayed in advertising by Canadian media . . . ." This task force was comprised of members of the advertising industry and public-sector representatives of recognized feminist organizations.

Public-sector task force members developed a consensus of concerns based on research studies from the last ten years, which showed that many advertisements are considered insulting to women. These concerns included: manner of portrayal to sexes, presence of sexes (e.g., predominance of male authority figures), use of sexual innuendos, and exclusion of ethnic and older women.

As part of the advertising industry response, the AAB agreed to set up a special Advisory Committee on Sex-Role Stereotyping. The Committee is responsible for an ongoing information and "sensitizing" program with industry associations and groups, supervision of public attitude research on related concerns, and handling of public complaints and counselling advertisers and advertising agencies.

For film, Committee guidelines, or complaints on sex-role stereotyping, contact:

Advertising Advisory Board
1240 Bay Street, Suite 305
Toronto, Ontario M5R 2A7
Phone: (416) 961-6311

or

Le Conseil des Normes de la Publicité
1499 rue de Bleury, Suite 200
Montréal, Québec H3A 2H5
Phone: (514) 849-5086

ACA and ICA

The Association of Canadian Advertisers is an organization that acts primarily as liaison between advertisers and government, helping in the selling, promoting, and marketing of products and services. For more information:

Association of Canadian Advertisers
180 Bloor St. West, Suite 1010
Toronto, Ontario M5S 2V6
Phone: (416) 964-3805

The Institute of Canadian Advertising is an association of advertising agencies acting on behalf of full-service advertising agencies. For more information:

Institute of Canadian Advertising
(L'Institut de la Publicité Canadienne)
8 King St. East, Suite 401
Toronto, Ontario M5C 1B5
Phone: (416) 368-2981

Over ten years ago, the joint boards of ACA and ICA funded a symposium in Toronto conducted by four eminent theologians. The published result of this symposium - *Truth in Advertising* (Toronto, 1973) - consists of guidelines "intended as a supplement to, and an extension of, the Canadian Code of Advertising Standards." Reprints are available from the Advertising Advisory Board.

Industry Codes and Guidelines

The Canadian Code of Advertising Standards is prepared and administered by the Advertising Standards Council, the self-regulatory arm of the Canadian advertising industry. The various clauses in the Code apply to all advertising and to all audio and visual media components. The various code clauses are supplementary to federal, provincial, and municipal legislation and regulations governing advertising. The principles underlying the Code and more detailed descriptions of its application are presented in *The Manual of General Guidelines For Advertising*.

The ASC also endorses in principle the International Code of Advertising Practice, developed by the International Chamber of Commerce and now adopted in some thirty countries.

The Advertising Standards Council and the regional Councils, which include public and business representatives, are autonomous bodies within their areas, established and funded by the advertising community to enforce voluntary codes of advertising standards.

Copies of this Code may be obtained by writing to any of the ASC addresses listed previously.

If you see or hear advertising carried by Canadian media that you feel contravenes one of the industry codes, write to the Advertising Standards Council nearest you. (The Councils, of course, have no control over advertising carried by non-Canadian media.) If it is a print advertisement, it helps if you can enclose a copy of the advertisement; with a broadcast message, give the station, approximate time, the name of the product, and why you think the message contravenes the Code.

Your complaint will be acknowledged and reviewed. If it appears the Code has been violated, Council staff will get in touch with the advertiser directly. In most cases corrective action follows. Where the advertiser disagrees with staff findings, the matter is referred to the full Council. If Council sustains the complaint, the advertiser is notified and asked to amend or withdraw the advertising. Generally, this closes the matter. Regardless of whether the complaint has been sustained or not, you will be notified of the outcome.

Occasionally an advertiser will refuse to take corrective action. The Council then notifies the media involved, or will sometimes ask that a bulletin be sent to all association members of those media, indicating that this message, in Council's judgement, contravenes the Code. In effect, this means media will not accept the message in its existing form.

Other Codes

Broadcast Code for Advertising to Children. Copies may be obtained from any of the ASC addresses listed, or from:

Canadian Association of Broadcasters
P.O. Box 627, Station B
Ottawa, Ontario K1P 5S2

Inquiries and comments about the Code, and complaints regarding alleged violations, should be made to:

(English commercials)
The Children's Advertising Section
Advertising Standards Council
1240 Bay Street, Suite 302
Toronto, Ontario M5R 2A7

(French commercials)
Le comité et la publicité destinée aux enfants
Counseil des Normes de la Publicité
Tele-Metropole (Canal 10)
CP 170 Succursale "C"
1600 est, boul. de Maisonneuve
Montréal, P.Q. H2L 4P6

Code of Advertising Standards, Association of Canadian Distillers. The members of the Association of Canadian Distillers firmly believe that they must be socially responsible and responsive to social change. They also believe, as advertisers, that they must ensure that their advertising demonstrates a sense of this social responsibility.

In the event of grievances relative to the Advertising Code, the Executive Committee of the Association of Canadian Distillers will answer any enquiries and examine and adjudicate any complaints. Write to:

Association of Canadian Distillers
350 Sparks Street, Suite 506
Ottawa, Ontario K1R 7S8

Television Code of Standards for Advertising Feminine Sanitary Protection Products. This code has been created by the Canadian Association of Broadcasters in co-operation with advertisers, their advertising agencies, the Telecaster Committee, and the ASC, which administers the code. Copies of this code in either English or French may be obtained from the Canadian Association of Broadcasters, the Advertising Standards Council in Toronto, or Le Conseil des Normes de la Publicité.

Advertising of Alcoholic Beverages: Provincial Liquor Control Boards. No advertising of alcohol products is allowed in Prince Edward Island, New Brunswick, and Saskatchewan. In all other provinces, only print and outdoor advertising of liquor products is permitted. Broadcast advertising of beer, wine, and cider products is permitted only in Alberta, Manitoba, Newfoundland, Nova Scotia, Ontario, Northwest Territories, and Yukon.

Any advertising of these products must have script clearance by the appropriate provincial liquor board and mandatory CRTC approval, which includes approval from the Department of Consumer and Corporate Affairs as well as approval by CBC Commercial Acceptance and by the Telecaster Committee, depending on stations used. For more information contact the liquor license board in your province.

Food and Drug Advertising: Department of National Health and Welfare. No commercial advertising an article marketed under the Propriety or Patent Medicine Act or the Food and Drugs Act may be accepted for broadcast scheduling by stations until it has been reviewed by either the Department of National Health and Welfare or the Department of Consumer and Corporate Affairs, is approved by the CRTC, and bears a registration number assigned by the CRTC. For more information, contact the Department of National Health and Welfare.

Suggested Reading

There are many books about advertising in the United States, few on the subject in Canada. I have listed some for you here that I have found helpful or entertaining.

Aristophanes. *Lysistrata.* Various editions.

Canadian Advertising Advisory Board. *Manual of general guidelines for advertising.* Toronto, 1975.

Caples, John. *How to Make Your Advertising Make Money.* Englewood Cliffs, N.J., 1983.

Della Femina, Jerry. *From those wonderful folks who gave you Pearl Harbor: front-line dispatches from the advertising war.* Edited by Charles Sopkin. New York, 1970.

Flesch, Rudolph. *The Art of Plain Talk.* Foreword by Lyman Bryson. New York, 1946.

Goodis, Jerry. *Have I Ever Lied to You Before.* Foreword by Peter C. Newman. Toronto, 1972.

Key, Wilson Bryan. *Subliminal Seduction.* Englewood Cliffs, N.J., 1973.

Lazar, Avrim, and Associates. *Advertising - Canada - Public Opinion. Attitudes of Canadians toward advertising on television.* Prepared for the Research Branch of the Canadian Radio-Television and Telecommunications Commission. Ottawa, 1978.

Lois, George, and Bill Pitts. *The Art of Advertising: George Lois on mass communication.* New York, 1977.

Morrissey, Mary. *Women and Advertising: a study of the opinions of Nova Scotian women regarding the portrayal of women in Canadian media advertising.* Prepared for the Nova Scotia Human Rights Commission. Halifax, 1979.

Ogilvy, David. *Ogilvy on Advertising.* New York, 1983.

Packard, Vance Oakley. *The Hidden Persuaders.* New York, 1967.

Reeves, Rosser. *Reality in Advertising.* New York, 1961.

Roman, Kenneth, and Joel Raphaelson. *Writing That Works.* New York, 1981.

Strunk, William, Jr., and E. B. White. *The Elements of Style.* New York, 1964.

Truth in Advertising. A Toronto School of Theology Symposium. Toronto, 1973.

Updegraff, Robert. *The Power of the Obvious: based on the business classic Obvious Adams.* Littleton, New Hampshire, 1916.

Acknowledgements

I would never have started this women's guide to advertising without the urging of Ethel Teitelbaum and the seminal idea from Colleen Dimson. Early research was pursued by Elizabeth Irwin. Carol Pollack found statistics for me and typed the first draft from my erratic handwriting. Later, she took a crack at editing the amorphous thing that I produced. I used much of her editing help.

Susan Robbins nursed me through my second draft, retyping and updating until she abandoned me to enter a course in public relations. Her successor, Pat Dunn, took up the flame. Micheline Tremblay assembled the details of the reading list for me and ploughed through rules and regulations to give you some idea in the Appendix of the morass of regulations that keep you safe from advertising. Helen, the woman I live with and to whom I am married, has provided invaluable assistance by not reading, criticizing, or correcting the grammar in any part of this book. She allowed me the peace and quiet on weekends and vacations to perform the almost impossible task (for one whose entire writing career has thus far entailed thirty-second commercials and one-page advertisements) of writing an entire book.